Black Religion / Womanist Thought / Social Justice
Series Editors Dwight N. Hopkins and Linda E. Thomas
Published by Palgrave Macmillan

A Womanist Pastoral Theology against Intimate and Cultural Violence

Stephanie M. Crumpton

First published in 2014 by
PALGRAVE MACMILLAN®
in the United States—a division of St. Martin's Press LLC,
175 Fifth Avenue, New York, NY 10010.

Where this book is distributed in the UK, Europe and the rest of the world,
this is by Palgrave Macmillan, a division of Macmillan Publishers Limited,
registered in England, company number 785998, of Houndmills,
Basingstoke, Hampshire RG21 6XS.

Palgrave Macmillan is the global academic imprint of the above companies
and has companies and representatives throughout the world.

Palgrave® and Macmillan® are registered trademarks in the United States,
the United Kingdom, Europe and other countries.

ISBN: 978–1–137–37813–2

Library of Congress Cataloging-in-Publication Data

Crumpton, Stephanie M., 1976–
    A womanist pastoral theology against intimate and cultural
violence / Stephanie M. Crumpton.
      pages cm
    Includes bibliographical references and index.
    ISBN 978–1–137–37813–2 (alk. paper)
      1. Violence—Religious aspects—Christianity. 2. African Americans—
Religion. 3. Womanist theology. 4. Black theology. 5. Feminist theology.
I. Title.

BR563.N4C79 2014
261.8'327082—dc23   2014013281

A catalogue record of the book is available from the British Library.

Design by Newgen Knowledge Works (P) Ltd., Chennai, India.

First edition: October 2014

10 9 8 7 6 5 4 3 2 1

To God—the Eternal Spirit who offers us time, energy, and opportunity to right things that have been wrong for far too long. Thank you Helen and Arthur McCullough, and Margaret, Isaiah, and Michael Crumpton for your ancestral presence along this journey. You nurtured the creativity and compassion that course through the veins of this project.

Contents

Acknowledgments

I first want to acknowledge my parents, Janis McCullough and Wayne P. Crumpton. I love you both very much. I have also been blessed with an incredibly supportive family—which includes many friends: Malu F. Fairley, Omar King, Catherine Booth, AnneMarie Mingo, Eboni Marshall Turman, Alisha L. Jones, Aishah Shahidah Simmons, Matthew W. Williams, Susan S. Mitchell, Estelle E. Archibold, Gene Shanks, Davita A. McCallister and Omolara C. Williams McCallister, David A. Hooker, Bridget Piggue, Bridget Hector, Monica A. Coleman, Gregory C. Ellison (III), Larena S. Burno, Shani Hebert, Dessalina Day, Kemett J. Timms, Rodrick Smith, Marylene Whitehead, Shelly Spencer Fitzsimmons, Robin Beaman, Helen Crossley, Pearl and Cedric Crumpton, Donald Walton, Amos & Irene & Dana & Lorraine Pace, Susan and Solomon Young, Jennifer L. Simms, "Freedom" and Bettie, Trinity United Church of Christ in Chicago, IL, Bethany Congregational Church in Thomasville, GA, First Congregational Church in Atlanta, GA, and First Afrikan Presbyterian Church in Lithonia, GA. You have shown me friendship, commitment, truth, hospitality, community, and deep love throughout this journey and in many other seasons in my life.

I am thankful for the seasoned saints and scholars whose guidance and sheer brilliance have nurtured and inspired me to think with head and soul: Oleta and Henry Young, Jeremiah A. Wright Jr., Pamela A. Fox, Carolyn A. L. McCrary, Ronald Keys, Willie F. Godman, April C. Wells, Phillis I. Sheppard, Lee H. Butler Jr., Katie G. Cannon, Renita J. Weems, Eugene Robinson, Halisi Edwards-Stanton, John B. Blevins, Carol Pitts,

Deborah A. Mullen, Jacquelyn Grant, Maryanne Bellinger, Denise McClane Davison, Mark A. Lomax, Sarita Davis, and Itihari Toure. I owe a special thank you to Sharon Watson Fluker, with whom I shared my wonderings about doctoral studies over lunch one day, having no idea that it would lead to this. Sharon, thank you for the Fluker era at the Fund for Theological Education.

I am grateful to Pamela Cooper-White, Emmanuel Y. Lartey, and Marcia Y. Riggs for believing that I had an idea worth pursuing and for investing their time, energy, and resources in my future as a scholar. Thank you for holding my feet to the fire and requiring that I grow.

Words cannot express how appreciative I am of Linda E. Thomas and Dwight N. Hopkins for acknowledging my work as worthy of being included in the Palgrave Macmillan series in Black Religion, Womanist Thought and Social Justice. I am humbled by the inclusion. Many thanks to Burke Gerstenschlager, religion editor at Palgrave, and his incredibly gracious assistant, Caroline Kracunas. I also owe a wealth of gratitude to Ulrike Guthrie who edited my work with expedience, skill, and kindness.

Finally...

I acknowledge and honor the six women who dared to speak and share their stories so that others may find words that would help us all be free. You, dear SisterFires, are golden.

Introduction

A Womanist Pastoral Theology against Intimate and Cultural Violence is about intimate violence and a culture that normalizes this violence in a particular way for Black females. Black girls and women experience overwhelming violence, and for many this violence begins while they are still young girls. The annual survey on intimate partner violence and sexual assault conducted by the Centers for Disease Control (CDC)[1] paints a clear portrait of two ugly truths in American society. The first is that for many, sexual violence has become a rite of passage of sorts into womanhood. The inaugural 2010 survey noted that over 21 million women reported that they had been raped at some point in their lives.[2] Of these, 29.9 percent were between eleven and seventeen years old the *first* time they were raped,[3] and this age was also the first time they recall being hit, slapped, kicked, or choked by someone with whom they were in a relationship.[4] The second ugly truth is that girls who experience sexual and physical abuse tend to experience more of the same kinds of violence in adulthood. One out of every five of the 21 million women interviewed was Black, and it is on this community that I focus in *A Womanist Pastoral Theology against Intimate and Cultural Violence*.

Large as they are, these numbers nonetheless fall short of capturing the full picture of violence against women in America because many choose not to report the violence, mostly out of fear. These women are among the millions of folks who fill church pews Sunday after Sunday. They are our mothers, partners, sisters, aunts, grandmothers, daughters, colleagues, and friends. In church and at home, their praise is often high and uplifted, and their prayers are profound and prolific. They worship, serve, and lead with everything within them. Through their worship and everyday moments of faith, they persevere against the psychological, spiritual, and physical memories of childhood sexual assault, molestation, incest, rape, battering/partner violence, and various other abuses. Yet, the institutional context of this faith, the church, oftentimes contributes to, justifies, and silences violence against girls and women.

The paradoxical nature of their relationship with the church has become an important area of interest. Within the last twenty years, women and men in religious and theological studies have named the church's complicity in this violence, and Black women have contributed distinct insights on the particularity of Black females' experience to the conversation.[5] While scholars have taken this crucial step to name the challenge, pastoral theological discourse has just recently begun to turn the corner on developing practices on the ground that are capable of responding to Black women's social, cultural, and religious particularity. The work has yet to connect with and influence the kind of systemic changes in faith communities that would make congregations a truly caring and transformative space for girls and women. This is a particularly tenuous reality for African American females who have traditionally contributed so much to the Black church movement for truth and justice, only to receive the stones of internalized racism, sexism, and disembodied theologies that can only compound the pain they already feel. Though lauded for its social legacy of communal freedom and justice, the Black church was and is not quite such a safe haven for Black female identities and bodies as it is sometimes portrayed.

The church is a primary contributor of psychological and moral messages that influence African American women's sense of humanity and according to Black psychologists like Nancy Boyd Franklin,[6] the church is one of the first places a good number of Black women will turn for help with intimate violence. But, the church does not always liberate and empower Black females against violence. While the Black church's political agenda espouses freedom and empowerment for all African

Americans, in reality freedom and empowerment for girls and women are often relegated to the margins. The practice of prioritizing race over and against gender establishes a double bind in the relationship Black girls and women have with the African American community. In the church, the effect of this double bind is evident in the lack of biblical interpretations, liturgies, and leadership paradigms that affirm females as made in the image of God, and as such, equals to males.

Even so, Black women in general, and Black women who have experienced intimate violence in particular, still affirm the church as a mainstay in their spirituality. The question is, why? Why do they cling to an institution whose practices and disembodying theologies fail to affirm all of who they are: Black and female? There has to be something more going on beneath the surface. I grew up in the Black church. I know firsthand the double-consciousness that Black women have to develop in order to participate in communities that we cherish, while also maintaining an important awareness that something is awry in these relationships. How do they manage the conflict? My instinct tells me that Black women are listening to and conferring authoritative status on subjugated and divergent voices that help them interrogate the double-binding nature of their relationship with the church, the African American community, and the wider cultural context.

In 2010 a small group of African American women answered my call to gather in Chicago to examine how they manage the conflict with institutions and relationships that both nourish and undermine them. It was the same year that the CDC launched an annual effort to survey and study the epidemic of sexual and physical assault. These women varied in age, education, employment, and sexual orientation. They were married, single, and partnered. What these mothers, daughters, sisters, and friends had in common was that they had broken their silences about intimate violence:[7] childhood sexual assault, molestation, incest, rape, and battering/partner violence. They shared deeply about the relationships and encounters that helped and hindered them at the time of the assault, and during their self-recovery, healing, and resistance. Their stories raised my awareness about how Black female healing from intimate violence is happening and that it is an incredibly complex process. Their healing was complex chiefly because it took place within the context of conversations and cultural spaces (including the church) that not only normalized violence against women in general (and women of color in particular) but also committed its own kind of violence. The processes and practices involved in their healing were not just about managing the posttraumatic symptoms of sexual and physical assault. They were also about the challenge of approaching this recovery within a cultural context that violated them through stereotypes and social processes that rendered them simultaneously invincible on one hand and inherently deserving of punishment on the other.

The women sensed this violent convergence and often responded to it by going within themselves and seeking out the sacred embrace of conversations and relationships that helped them name and interrogate not only their intimate pain but also the multiple cultural forces that compounded and indeed allowed that pain. These relationships and conversations equipped the women with wisdom and survival strategies to grapple with the meaning of intimate and cultural assault in light of their faith. The stories they shared with me provided a snapshot of Black women's experiences of intimate and cultural violence. These stories raised concerns over whether or not dominant existing paradigms for care are congruent with the ways and rhythms of how many Black women approach healing.

Their narratives drive the dialectic conversation that unfolds in the following chapters. Given the cultural, psychological, and theological themes that emerged in their narratives, I engage Black Feminist thought, Self psychology, and Womanist theology for concepts and analysis that help me name and address the underlying dynamics at play in the women's stories, dynamics to which pastoral theology must be attentive if it is going to be relevant.

A Black Feminist/Womanist Sociohistoric Perspective

Sociohistoric analysis by Black Feminists and Womanists places Black women's contemporary experience of intimate and cultural violence within a larger conversation about traditions that nor-malize violence against them. At issue is the historic deployment of stereotypes that keep racist, sexist, classist, and heteronorma-tive images of Black womanhood alive in the American cultural ethos and memory. In *Black Sexual Politics: African Americans, Gender and the New Racism* Patricia Hill Collins identifies three primary stereotypes of Black women: Mammy (the asex-ual/deferential caretaker); Jezebel (the manipulative seductress); and Sapphire (the angry, loud, aggressive matriarch).[8] Collins's claim is that these "controlling images" are contemporary re-presentations of persistent Enlightenment-era beliefs that categorize Black females as inherently self-sacrificing, immoral, sexually deviant, and angry.

Womanist ethicist Emilie Townes identifies the hegemonic imagination of White males in positions of power and influence, rather than Black women's real lived existence, as the source of these controlling images. Townes's analysis reveals that control-ling images emerged in public space at particular points in his-tory to preserve White male identity and morality at times when institutionalized racism and racialized sexual violence commit-ted against Black women was especially prominent. She begins with the Mammy image, which

from slavery through the Jim Crow era (1877–1966),...served the economic, political and social interests of White ideol-ogy and history in the United States. Her caricature was used to prove that Black women (and by extension children and men) were happy with their enslavement...Her construction is a response to abolitionist claims that slave owners sexually exploited their female slaves, especially light skinned ones. Mammy is constructed as an ugly antidote to such charges. After all, who would abuse a desexualized, fat, Black woman when the only other morally viable alternative was the idealized White woman. Mammy was not sexual or sensual—she was and is completely de-eroticized and safe. However, this safety did not extend to White women of the plantation South or Black women, children and men. The mammy provided safety for an idealized patriarchal White family structure—she pro-vided safety for White men.[9]

Referencing Melvin Patrick Ely, Townes next describes Sapphire as an electronic media creation:

> This media generated image of Black women that emerged in the 1930s and 1940s always portrayed Sapphire as obstinate, domineering and contemptuous of Black men...
>
> This image of the bitter, hostile, cold and domineering Black woman who is in-charge is dangerous to the White imagination. Whites had no "safe" place to put a Black woman who cared for her family, who had ideas and could articulate them, who did not relate to White culture—by choice, and who was fiercely protective of her family—keeping everyone (men included) in line, fed and cared for if that is what the situation demanded. This kind of Black woman was impossible for the White imagination to grasp or conjure. She is fully human, and as such, she had to be demonized to fit the worlds of blackness the White imagination sought to create. Ultimately, Sapphire is threatening to authority/hegemony.[10]

Townes extends her analysis to cover another era in the cultural production of controlling images, the Civil Rights–era Black matriarch:

> Before the 1960s, female-headed households were more common in Black communities. However, it is important to note that an ideology racializing female-headedness as a causal feature of Black poverty and moral depravity had not yet emerged. The Mammy is the Black mother figure in White homes; the Matriarch is the Black mother figure in Black homes. As Collins and Robin Good note, she is the bad Black mother who spends too much time away from her home working to support her family. In a twisted bit of logic, The Black Matriarch can also be the Mammy at the same time—proving that context and perception *are* important. Because she is single and works, she cannot supervise her children and this contributes to their failure in school and in society. She is single because she is overly aggressive and unfeminine. She emasculates her lovers and husbands who either refuse to marry her or desert her. How expedient— the perceived moral failures of Black children and Black men are placed, literally, in the laps of Black women. The Matriarch

opens the floodgates for social theorizing about the intergenerational character of Black poverty through the transmission of values in Black families.[11]

Townes's research reveals how lies told to cover over mixed race children as evidence of slave owners' rape of enslaved Black women (Mammy), the depiction of Black women as loud-mouthed and uncontrollable (Sapphire), and finally the hyper-sexualization of Black female poverty (Black matriarch/welfare queen/Jezebel) supply images which are in turn used to justify assaults committed against them.

Evelyn Brooks Higginbotham examines Black women's moral response to this cultural legacy, particularly the "politics of respectability" that emerged in response to controlling images that depicted Black women as inherently immoral. In *Righteous Discontent: The Women's Movement in the Black Baptist Church, 1880–1920,* Higginbotham notes that Black women deployed "manners and morals" as "resistant pronouncements against white public opinion of Black women as immoral, child-like and unworthy of respect or protection."[12] The initial intent was to disprove white lies of Black immorality by doing all they could in their attire, posture, speech, and behavior to demonstrate high moral values. Black women probably weren't aware (or could barely spare the energy to consider) the psychological consequences of presenting and maintaining this protective public image. The politics of respectability that Higginbotham described created a double bind in Black women's relationships with members of their own communities, as well as outside of African American circles. Take for instance Black women who were raped and assaulted by white male employers while doing domestic work. Disclosure would have made them vulnerable to dominant cultural beliefs that presumed Black women's sexual wantonness as the force that drove white men to rape them. In a more practical sense, crying out about sexual assault would often put them at risk of losing the job that put food in their children's mouths, or even of losing their lives. Besides, during the bellum, antebellum, and Jim/Jane Crow eras, what police would they call? The politics of respectability was real, and the double bind that came with it extended to Black girls' and women's experience of their own communities. Reporting abuse would have called their fidelity to the race into question, during a period in history when African Americans had to prioritize the survival of the community in the face of racial violence over the internal violence girls and women experienced from males in their own communities. In response, Black girls and women developed a subculture of their own that allowed them to navigate these double binds. Darlene Clark-Hine writes,

> Black women, as a rule, developed and adhered to a cult of secrecy, a culture of dissemblance, to protect the sanctity of inner aspects of their lives. The dynamics of dissemblance involved creating the appearance of disclosure, or openness about themselves and their feelings, while actually remaining an enigma. Only with secrecy, thus achieving a self-imposed invisibility, could ordinary Black women accrue the psychic space and harness the resources needed to hold their own in the often one-sided and mismatched resistance struggle.[13]

Clark-Hine's description offers powerful insight into the often unknown inner world of Black women. The difficulty, however, was that like the politics of respectability, it left few opportunities for the community to acknowledge and claim accountability for any role they may have had in the women's pain. The culture of dissemblance and the politics of respectability that Higginbotham articulates are two historic examples of strategies that Black girls and women developed to survive intimate violence and resist the insidious effects of cultural violence via controlling images. Black women continue to hand down these survivalist strategies (for better or worse) to contemporary Black girls and women who experience intimate and cultural violence today.

This kind of sociohistoric analysis allows us to set contemporary experience against a backdrop that helps us better understand how the cultural production of controlling images plays a role in Black women's experiences of intimate and cultural violence. This is a matter of concern for pastoral theology because the scripts embedded in these distorting images have powerful influence over how Black girls and women go about seeking care and support for their healing. These scripts conjure in women fear and apprehension about how, if, when, and to whom they can disclose intimate violence. The fear is whether or not justice-seeking disclosure (the antithesis of Mammyesque self-sacrificing) will result in communal backlash for outing their abusers, especially if the person is male, a family member, or an important figure in the community. The fear is whether or not proclaiming that she is a sexual victim (a clear antithesis of Jezebel's sexual wantonness) will reverse her circumstance, such that she becomes the scapegoat for both her abuser and the community that refuses to hold abusers accountable. The apprehension is also about how the decision to exercise her right not to press criminal charges and seek formal justice (the antithesis of Sapphire's unbridled, yet justified,rage) might render her weak in the eyes of those who believe that the measure of a Black woman is whether or not she will show up for the fight, regardless of the impact of the initial trauma, or the possibility of subsequent retraumatization that often occurs in criminal justice proceedings.[14]

We will see in the stories that follow that contemporary African American women's awareness of these historical dynamics can be seen in how the telling of their healing journey is shot through with concern over how they are perceived. As is the case with any woman, regardless of race, Black women are concerned with the emotional consequences of recalling traumatic events. However, sociohistoric analyses from Black feminist and Womanist thinkers help us to see the distinction in how Black women are also concerned with whether or not it is socially permissible for them to seek help, whether telling their stories will simply continue to validate stereotypes as truths that justify the abuse they experienced, or whether breaking the silence can bring about change and healing

Self Psychology on Intimate and Cultural Violence

The sociohistoric circumstances that Black Feminists and Womanists bring into view clarify the interrelated nature of intimate and cultural violence. Therapeutic response requires us to focus on the intrapsychic consequences of these co-occurring dynamics. By intrapsychic I mean the complex unconscious and semiconscious processes that influence a woman's sense of herself as a cohesive, continuous self whose identity forms in response to intrapsychic dynamics with others. When these inter-actions include childhood sexual assault, molestation, incest, rape, battering/partner violence and stereotypes that normalize these assaults in a particular way for Black girls and women, trauma is bound to persist. Three concepts from Self psychologi-cal theory—selfobject, empathy, and cultural selfobject—offer a framework for conceptualizing psychological development, intrapsychic trauma, and culture as focal points in caring and counseling responses to intimate and cultural violence.

In Self psychological perspective, intrapsychic development and growth take place in a shared relational context in which interpersonal encounters provide emotional exchanges that either promote or distort personality development. While the theory asserts that the personality's core forms in infancy, it also affirms that personalities continue to develop throughout life, and that interactions with others are critical components in this ongoing process. The early architect of the theory, Heinz Kohut, developed the "selfobject" concept to describe the impact of relational contexts on intrapsychic development:

> Selfobjects are objects which we experience as part of our self; the expected control over them is, therefore, closer to the concept of the control which a grown-up expects to have over others. There are two kinds of selfobjects: those who respond to and confirm the child's innate sense of vigour, greatness and perfection and those to whom the child can look up and with whom he can merge as an image of calmness, infallibility and omnipotence. The first one is referred to as the mirror-ing selfobject, the second as the idealized parent image. The self, the core of our personality, has various constituents which we acquire in the interplay with those persons in our earliest childhood environment whom we experience as selfobjects.[15]

Kohut envisioned the mother as the primary, mirroring self-object in a dyadic configuration with the infant, and the father as the primary idealizing selfobject at a later time in the child's development. The infant's narcissistic experience of selfobjects constitutes a form of transference in which the child experiences others as a part of her own self, rather than as an interdependently related other. In optimal nurturing environments caregivers take practical actions and offer affective responses to narcissistic transference that support the developmental maturation away from primal, need-seeking connections, toward interdependent, reciprocal connections with others. When selfobjects fail to provide empathic resonance as the platform for psychological growth, the personality that develops remains centrally organized around narcissistic need-seeking behaviors. In Self psychological perspective, this failure creates a form of trauma.

When the early parenting environment fails to provide empathic resonance, or worse, if members in the caretaking context abuse the dependent child, the traumatic experience influences intrapsychic development. Protective defenses of repression, dissociation, and disavowal enacted to fend off immensely threatening empathic failures can become organizing elements around which a narcissistically ordered personality develops. In a sense, these defenses become a primary, intrapsychic program that informs the individual's approach and response to all interpersonal encounters. Kohut initially developed Self psychological theory to grapple with care for people whose personalities were centrally organized around these intrapsychic defenses. From a classic analytic perspective, affective instability, cycles of idealization and subsequent devaluation, and intense stay-leave behaviors prompted by intrapsychic defenses that characterize narcissistically organized personalities prevent transference between client and therapist. However, Kohut recognized the enactment of these defenses as a form of transference in and of itself. This narcissistic transference became more apparent and seemed to intensify when he focused on the emotional content of experience, rather than fact-finding and interpretation, in conversations with clients. The therapeutic alliance strengthened when he mirrored back the client's affect and followed up with carefully timed conveyance that he *felt* what the client re-presented in the counseling session. He defined this as the process of facilitating *empathy*, in which the client takes in the counselor's mature psychological structure via transmuting internalization to reinforce an inner sense of cohesion and continuity. Facilitating empathy (rather than fact-finding about painful events and encounters) as a response to traumatic transference proved to be the missing element in the connection process. Over time, he noticed growth in the clients' capacity to demonstrate empathy toward their own selves, which subsequently transformed the narcissistic nature of their transference in therapy as well as their connection-seeking behaviors outside of the therapeutic context. Empathy functioned to support development that allowed intrapsychic defenses to recede.

Self psychology's understanding of empathy's function in healing adds much to this project's focus on developing therapeutic response to the intrapsychic consequences of empathically failing events like childhood sexual abuse, molestation, rape, incest, and battering/partner violence and cultural violence. I turn to Self psychological theory as a useful framework for working through traumatic transference resulting from intimate violence because, though its origin may differ, traumatic transference is often similar in its presentation to narcissistic transference.[16] In order for Self psychology to provide a tool that opens up rather than distorts understandings of Black women's ongoing development, the theory requires some adjustments. Womanist pastoral theologian and Self psychoanalyst Phillis I. Sheppard explains, "The self cannot be excised from the social milieu, and moreover, this social context gives rise to a gendered cultural, sexual and racial/ethnic self."[17] This means that concepts of race, gender, sexuality, and class are embedded in the empathic or empathically failing responses that self-objects provide. It also means that practitioners must first consider the social and cultural biases present in the theory before applying it as a viable lens for reading Black female experience. Sheppard critiques Kohut's conceptualization of psychological development "where social location, race and gender are never named as integral to the theory because the self is assumed to be white or at least like white, male or like male, and confident in the dominant social milieu."[18] While Kohut was clear in his assumption about the impact of unempathic relational milieus on development, he stopped short of considering how social and cultural oppression are pathogenic factors at play in contact between individuals, communities, and institutions that constitute the shared relational context within which all psychological development take places.

The theory's lack of attention to cultural and social dynamics also plays out in understandings of who is a part of the caregiving contexts that influence psychological growth and ongoing development. Kohut's caregiving framework between mother and child presumes a woman in partnership with a male parent. This configuration suggests an underlying focus on the nuclear family and accompanying heteronormative assumptions. In so doing it fails to acknowledge single parents, same-gender loving parents, multigenerational models of child rearing, and extended family networks (including grandparents, fictive kin, and non–birth parents) in its understanding of primary caregiving contexts. The diversity of Black women's families of origin and parents, as well as their own partnering/parenting choices requires critique and revision of the theory, so that in its application, clinicians and care providers may fully engage their social and cultural particularity.

One more concept from Self psychological theory deserves attention in developing a framework that examines the influence of culture on intrapsychic development. Kohut's cultural self-object conceptualizes how art/culture and prominent public figures facilitate empathy on behalf of the communities they represent, including communities of individuals who hold negative views of Black female embodiment. Kohut initially defined cultural self-objects as "the replica of the culture for the group self of what occurs in individual development."[19] Cultural selfobjects emerge out of groups of selves to meet the groups' needs for empathic connections with mirroring figures who support their collective sense of cohesion and continuity. Cultural selfobjects also create opportunities for groups of selves to identify and connect with important ideals. In an article titled "Idealization and Cultural Selfobjects," Kohut writes,

> One needs to be accepted and mirrored—there has to be the gleam in some mother's eye which says it is good that you are here and I acknowledge your being here and I am uplifted by your presence. There is also the other need: to have somebody strong and knowledgeable and calm around with whom I can temporarily merge, who will uplift me when I am upset. Originally, that is an actual uplifting of the baby by the mother; later that becomes an uplifting feeling of looking at a great man or woman and enjoying him or her, of following in his or her footsteps, of a great idea being uplifting, or a wonderful piece of music, etc. That is extremely important. And when I talked about cultural selfobjects, which is the replica of the culture for the group self of what occurs in individual development, I think that these two basic needs are also present, perhaps collectively.[20]

Cultural selfobjects are the ideals, the creative artistic mediums, and the public figures who mirror back our value in ways that make us feel uplifted. As with the selfobject, the need for sustaining connections with mirroring cultural selfobjects persists throughout life as a critical dimension in ongoing psychological growth and development. Like all people, in order to thrive, Black women need to experience great women, men, and ideals in community and society as mirroring cultural selfobjects with whom they connect and experience a sense of uplift that affirms them and supports psychological health.

If that is the case, what then are the intrapsychic consequences of Black women's historic experience of racist, sexist, classist, and heteronormative projections embedded in certain cultural selfobjects? Sheppard writes,

> Like the concept selfobject, Kohut assumed cultural selfobjects to be sources of self cohesion brought about via the engagement with cultural productions such as art, important figures, literature, music, and so on. Thus, he held that cultural selfobjects served to facilitate self cohesion for the individual and for

groups. However, Kohut's use of the concept failed to adequately address aspects of society including cultural productions and experiences that undermine self cohesion as well as how negative experiences are sometimes used by individuals and groups to serve to enhance self-esteem and cohesion.[21]

As Sheppard points out, cultural selfobjects are not only individuals who operate in public space like certain artists, celebrities, politicians, socialites, community leaders, or other public figures. Rather, cultural selfobjects are also the "symbols, language, institutions and cultural productions"[22] that meet the mirroring and idealizing needs of the groups they represent. Sheppard's critique also raises awareness about negative consequences for self-development when groups of selves project disavowed aspects of themselves onto others in order to maintain self-esteem and cohesion. An example would be the controlling images of Black women that Townes traces back to White males' efforts to preserve White male identity and morality. Other mediums include cultural rhetoric that "suppresses human potential,"[23] institutions that secure privilege for some while denying it to others, artistic productions that esteem some humanities by devaluing others, and public figures who symbolize abusive uses of power and privilege. Each of these mediums function as cultural selfobjects that contribute negative psychic material to the shared relational context within which Black women's self-development occurs.

While these cultural selfobjects certainly show up in culturally produced stereotypes emerging out of other groups to depict Black women as loud-mouthed (the Sapphire) and self-sacrificing (the Mammy), some of these cultural selfobjects emerge out of the African American community's own "self" as a result of its intragroup struggles with colorism, sexism, classism, and homophobia. In these instances, the psychological stakes are higher for Black girls and women who encounter language as a cultural selfobject present in the conversations that they have with members of their own communities. One such example is language in which words like "strong" are used to laud Black women's resilience, without acknowledging the dehumanizing way in which this descriptor portrays them as invincible in the face of death-dealing circumstances. Concerning cultural selfobjects that emerge from other group selves that negatively impact Black female experience, it is also important to notice public policy agendas as cultural selfobjects. Public policy agendas that negatively impact the economic circumstance of Black mothers, as Townes analysis points out, are often motivated by policymakers' unacknowledged moral assumptions about Black female sexuality.[24] Analyzing the psychic material embedded in these cultural selfobjects and others sheds light on the intrapsychic impact of racism, classism, sexism, and homophobia on Black women.

Self psychology helps me identify the psychic material that is embedded in the shared relational and cultural context within which Black female self-development occurs. The theory also provides a useful framework for thinking through how counseling can function as a context in which clients may experience empathic resonance that nurtures, affirms, and empowers them to heal from intrapsychic wounds created by multiple forms of violence.

Womanist God-Talk

Womanist pastoral theology takes seriously the predicament Black women encounter when trying to find God in the face of emotional, physical, sexual, cultural, and spiritual pain. Womanist theologians Delores S. Williams and Kelly Brown Douglas examine the church's role in this struggle in ways that I find helpful for this project. With matters concerning African American health, sexuality, and wholeness in mind, their respective analysis of classic views of the incarnation and the atonement sheds light on the church as a mediator of Christian traditions that impact how Black women think about their bodies and the role of suffering in their relationship with God. Their analysis and critique revisit the path to claim the ontological goodness of human flesh and the sacredness of Black female embodiment (inclusive of sexuality) in light of traditions that valorize suffering—two theological concerns that must be addressed if any real work is to be done to help women heal.

Douglas asks: How we can value the Christ's enfleshed reality and the subsequent meaning made of his bodily crucifixion? Was Jesus's flesh, its emotional and corporeal realities, and cultural experience an integral part of the incarnation? Or, was his flesh an antagonistic hindrance? Something to be overcome through suffering on a cross in order that the fullness of the incarnation might come to pass.

In *Sexuality and the Black Church: A Womanist Perspective* Douglas questions whether or not religious intellectuals and pastoral practitioners operate from an understanding of God's incarnation through Jesus that empowers them to actively respond to the crisis in African American health and sexuality.[25] Rather than speak of the incarnation in disembodied terms that skip over the implications of God's revelation through Jesus' embodied existence, Douglas argues that "the incarnation indicates that God is embodied in human history through Jesus Christ and, as such, is an intimately active presence in the lives of women and men."[26]

Douglas's analysis demonstrates how disembodied views of the incarnation depreciate the human body by insinuating "that though God was revealed in Jesus, the embodiment was only incidental to the actual divine revelation in Jesus. They do not take seriously the radical meaning of the incarnation, that God was in fact *en sarki* (in the flesh)."[27] Interpretive traditions based on disembodied views of the incarnation presume that, to exist in the flesh is to take on a physical existence that is inherently antagonistic to intimacy with God. This primary argument translates into the classic theological disposition that sin is ontological and that flesh is unequivocally synonymous with sinfulness.

From her own perspective as an Anglican priest and feminist pastoral theologian, Pamela Cooper-White explains,

> Even within the metaphorical account of the Fall, the goodness of creation was primary and included human beings. God saw what God had made and declared everything "very good"

(Gen. 1:31). Before there was original sin, there was original goodness and "original blessing." The human being was and is created in God's image (Gen. 1:26). Before any doctrine of original sin, there was original goodness. Sin is a condition of woundedness, alienation from God and from others in creation, but goodness is prior.[28]

Cooper-White's assertion supports Douglas's move to claim the ontological goodness of human flesh. Douglas's embodied view of the incarnation dislocates the genesis of sin from the flesh to locate it in the systemic cultural and institutional processes that wound, ignore, disempower, and oppress minds, bodies, and spirits. An embodied view of the incarnation is foundational for us to recognize "body-denying and death-dealing"[29] rhetoric that influences how women value their distinctly Black and female flesh, and how they reckon with damage done to this flesh. It is also significant because this rhetoric offers hooks on which to hang psychological analysis of the church's impact on identity as an important cultural selfobject influencing Black women's ongoing psychological development.

A second step in understanding the theological complexities involved in Black women's faith in light of violence concerns classic Christian ideas about what actually took place when Jesus's body was crucified. In *Sisters in the Wilderness: The Challenge of Womanist God Talk*,[30] Williams examines the implications of classic doctrines of the atonement on Black women considering their historic experiences of enslavement, forced surrogacy, and servitude to White owners and employers. She is concerned with the impact of classic atonement theories on Black women who consider atonement a point of reference for making sense of God's regard for them in light of their oppression. Classic ransom and moral and substitution doctrines of atonement locate humanity's redemption in Jesus's suffering and death on the cross as a surrogate for humankind. Williams deconstructs these doctrines and reveals the painful implications they can have for communities struggling to reconcile collective experiences of institutionalized surrogacy with notions about the saving work of Jesus's surrogacy.

Her analysis examines the particular sociopolitical and cultural context that informed the theological language used to articulate theories of atonement. In her deconstruction she reminds us that all language is deeply embedded in the social, political, and cultural themes that dominate particular historical contexts and she examines the particular sociopolitical and cultural context that informed the theological language that have been used to articulate classic theories of atonement. She reminds us that whether in the case of Origen and Anselm's theories of atonement, Abelard's moral theory of atonement, or Calvin's substitution theory of atonement, each writer articulated his ideas "in the language and thought that people of a particular time understood and in which they were grounded."[31] In her reading of Origen she observes how his conceptualization of Jesus's death on the cross as a "ransom God paid to the devil for the sins of humankind"[32] reflected first-century culture's preoccupation with devils and spirits, chivalry and dishonor. Writing during the Middles Ages, an era characterized by the church's stress on the penitential life of believers, Abelard's theory of atonement conceptualized Christ's surrogacy in terms of its moral implication for humankind. Subsequently, Calvin's work in the Reformation period emphasized the primacy of ancient law, which evidenced itself in the judicial language he used to speak of Christ's surrogacy.

Each of the atonement theories they developed and the language they used to articulate it emerged out of the cultural norms that influenced their experience of social location. With this language history in mind, Williams then asks us to imagine what theological language might emerge when Black women articulate claims about the meaning of Jesus's suffering on the cross in light of their social location. She also pushes Womanist religious scholars to engage a constructive process in which the

> ...womanist theologian uses the sociopolitical thought and action of the African-American woman's world to show black women their salvation does not depend upon any form of surrogacy made sacred by traditional and orthodox understandings

of Jesus' life and death. Rather their salvation is assured by Jesus' life of resistance and by the survival strategies he used to help people survive the death of identity caused by their exchange of inherited cultural meanings for a new identity shaped by the gospel ethics and worldview.[33]

Rather than accept classic theories of atonement, Williams puts forth a "constructive Womanist concept of salvation"[34] in which Christ's redemptive power is located in his focus on rejecting defiling sociopolitical processes. Christ's life—not his surrogate death—redeems humankind. His life and ministry are replete with examples of systemic transformation of dehumanizing practices and structures that defile individuals and communities, including Black women. His life and ministry also offer alternatives to Black women's participation or complicity in practices and structures that defile them. Salvation, then, lies in large part in the transformation of sociopolitical structures that "defile the balance between the material and the spiritual, between life and death, between power and the exertion of it."[35] In stark contrast to atonement theories that locate salvation in the suffering of the crucifixion, Williams locates salvation in God's resurrecting power that transforms political and cultural systems like racism, sexism, classism, ageism, and all kinds of violence that defile minds, bodies, and souls. Salvation is about restoring balance, affirming the image of God in all human beings, and working toward micro- and macrolevel encounters that support this affirmation.

Womanist theology provides a sociohistoric theological framework that acknowledges the spiritual nature of the damage done when Black women are assaulted physically, sexually, and psychologically through intimate and cultural violence. Douglas and Williams's critiques highlight deleterious elements within classic Christian theology that significantly inform church traditions. Taken together, their constructive moves toward embodied views of the incarnation and redemption through social/cultural transformation offer lenses that allow us to see more clearly the tensions that are present in Black women's faith lives as well as the ways they move through these tensions to connect with God through the everydayness of life.

The Road Ahead...

The dialectic between the firsthand narratives shared by the women I interviewed, Black feminist thought, Self psychology, and womanist theology brought forth three questions that orient this book:

1. Is there a match between contemporary/current models of care and the ways women approach survival and practice healing?
2. Does pastoral theological methodology go far enough in its provision of tools that support professionals in developing cultural competency around their own, as well as Black women's, experience of cultural violence?
3. Is contemporary pastoral theology positioned to engage the religious pluralism that shows up in Black syncretic spirituality?

A response to these questions and others unfolds in the following chapters based on the premise that intimate and cultural violence are traumas that have intrapsychic and spiritual consequences to which practitioners must be attentive if they are to do sound care with Black women.

Chapter 1: "I Can Speak for Myself" shares the actual words that "Rori," "Eliza," "Camille," "Tamara," "Cirene," and "Octavia"[36] used to talk about what they experienced, how they felt, who mattered and how they "made it through" experiences of intimate and cultural violence. Collectively, their words provide points of departure for pastoral theological discourse and practices of care and counseling that make sense for who and how many Black women understand themselves in the world.

Chapter 2: "Navigating the Hostile Terrain of Intimate and Cultural Violence" examines the intrapsychic consequences of violence and the psychological material found in personal relationships and social encounters that helped or hindered self-recovery from intimate and cultural violence. I explore the developmental impact of childhood intimate violence on adult intimacy and sexuality and focus on supports that helped women expose and interrogate hostile attitudes about race, gender, sexuality, and class that can only exacerbate the intrapsychic consequences of intimate violence. They responded to this hostility by seeking out relationships, experiences, encounters, images, and messages that nurtured them, provided practical support, and equipped them to counter social attitudes that normalized violence committed against them. While it is clear that these relationships were lifesaving, I examine how the lifesaving quality of these connections is rooted in the psychological resources they lend to healing from intrapsychic trauma.

Chapter 3: "A God I Recognize" examines intimate violence and cultural assault as abuse that impacts Black women spiritually. The chapter discusses how the women wrestled with a sense of alienation from God, self, and others in the wake of violence. It presents narratives of their direct and indirect encounters with God, the various ways they interrogated their theological heritage to actively seek out a God they could recognize, a reconstructed spirituality that engaged multiple faith traditions, and embodied spiritual practices through which they experienced a connection with God that strengthened them holistically (in mind, body, and spirit).

Chapter 4: "WomanistCare: Reshaping Images and Paradigms for Care" examines how pastoral response that resonates with the ways Black women approach self-recovery and healing requires new images and paradigms for care. I respond to this need by introducing *working images of WomanistCare* that prompt pastoral theological reflection on norms for care, and practitioners' cultural countertransference responses to Black women. Next, a case study of WomanistCare ritual is presented for analysis and reflection on ritual as a congregation-based, communal act of care with women. Analysis includes discussion of the use and abuse of power in ritual space convened to meet the needs of women who have experienced violence.

Chapter 5: "Womanist Pastoral Counseling: Clinical Considerations" explores psychodynamic counseling response to intrapsychic struggles stemming from childhood sexual abuse, molestation, incest, rape, battering/partner violence and a cultural context that normalizes these offenses. Traumatic sequelae (aftereffects) of intimate violence are detailed, and Kohutian ideas on the use of empathy to work through traumatic transference and shame are also addressed. Ways in which Black women's spirituality as an everyday strategy for healing can be integrated as a resource in the therapeutic process are also highlighted.

I close the discussion with concluding notes on self-care and thoughts about the work that lies ahead in pastoral theology's discourse and practical responses to violence.

I Can Speak (the Unspeakable) for Myself

The stories shared in this chapter are taken directly from transcripts of group and one-on-one interviews with six women, the chapter also includes excerpts from written narratives they provided. All but one of the women were children under eleven years old the first time they experienced intimate violence, and the person who abused them was a member of their immediate or extended family. These women reflect diversity in age, education, employment, and sexual orientation. They are married, single, partnered, mothers, daughters, friends, and sisters who shared deeply with me about their inner lives and the encounters and relationships that helped and/or hindered them.

The chapter presents the words that women I am calling Rori, Eliza, Camille, Tamara, Cirene, and Octavia[1] used to talk about what they experienced, how they felt, who mattered, and how they "made it through." Collectively, their words provide points of departure for those who do pastoral care and counseling to learn how many Black women grapple with violence and understand themselves in the world.

Rori

"It's All Coming…But It Got to Pass"

With her broad smile and curious eyes, the group came to expect Rori to be the one who would bring a sense of humor to the conversation. She told us that laughter was one of the ways she deals with what happened to her. Humor helped her speak the truth about being sexually abused by a church elder who was also a member of her extended family. He abused her and her sisters for about three years until an aunt caught wind of it and intervened:

> Okay. Where do I begin? I'm a sister of three other sisters. But, it was like three of us was three stair-steps. And being raised in the church all my life, a lot of people laugh at me because I always compare everything to sex. But, that's all I've ever known. As a little girl, I remember being molested by a man we call, on the outside, Uncle [name omitted], but at church, "Elder [last name omitted]," who is a minister (his wife was like our godmother).
>
> What they would do... (I still to this day don't understand how my mother who sees all [did] not see that this man was molesting her three daughters).
>
> I remember as a little girl he would dress us all up as little baby dolls. And it wasn't him [sic]. His wife would be at some white lady's house doing house work. And he would have us in his car. And I remember I would be the one that he would sit on the roof of the car. Both sisters would be on the front seat with the door open, legs open, panties down. And the sister that's under me would be in the backseat, panties down. And I can remember (every time I see Vaseline now, I get these flashbacks). I can remember him with a baby nipple on his finger. And he would dip it into the Vaseline. And he would just do whatever. I remember him taking his penis out sometime. If he put me in the backseat with the door open and had one of the others someplace else... I remember him rubbing his penis up against my vagina. I remember all of that.
>
> And then when we finally told our mother that Uncle [name omitted] was playing with my "tookie"(because at that time she told us it was a "tookie"). [She said] "No. Don't be lying on Uncle [name omitted]. Don't lie on him." And for the longest, that happened, like for three years. Because I remember from three to five. And then finally my auntie heard about it. She said, "He did what?" So then she went and confronted my mother. She said as a child she was molested by her brothers. So, she knows... "Those children just didn't make that up." And, [she said] you need to get them away from him.

So, by that time my father got wind of it. And this guy would just show up. He would try to wrestle with my mother to try to get his rocks off some kind of way. And I remember my father going between…He had chased him out of our apartment. And he was stretched across from this apartment building to the other apartment building trying to get to this man. Because he had come out of our bathroom window and was stretched across to somebody else's apartment trying to get them to let him in so he could get away.

Rori's experience was horrific, and the situation was made even more difficult by the fact that the church, a significant part of her family's identity and spirituality, was also the place where she regularly encountered her abuser. Looking back, she concluded that she and her sisters weren't alone. She believed that there were more girls, other than just her sisters, on whom this same man had also preyed:

> Everything else that happened in my life happened with the confusion of the sex and spirituality. I mean, the sex and church. Church and sex. It took me a long time to, and I still work on that, to separate the two. Because that's just there. It's just thrown in your face and you see the damage that was done. All these young ladies were there at this church. All of them got these same confused thoughts.

Rori's confusion about sex and spirituality began in childhood, but the effects of the violence she experienced showed up later in her adult relationships. She recalled,

> I had tickets to a Peabo Bryson concert. I was so happy. I *sang* "Feel the Fire" with Peabo Bryson. I sang the female parts in all of his songs. After the show, my girlfriend dropped me off at the apartment that Mr. Wonderful and I shared. I took the elevator up to the fourth floor, walked to the apartment door, put my key [in] the lock and said, "Honey, I'm home." To my surprise, Mr. Hyde appeared from behind the door and said, "Where you been Bitch?" I had never heard him speak to me that way before. As I looked up at him through drunken eyes I never saw it coming. He hit me upside my head with his opened hand. I felt like

I had been hit with the door. The room was dark but I actually saw *stars*. I screamed as he began to hit me and punch me like I was a punching bag. I balled myself up in a knot and attempted to protect what parts of me that had not been punched. I got myself together enough to get my keys to my car and run out of the apartment.

The violence caught her off guard and it made a lasting impression on her emotionally, psychologically, and even spiritually. During the initial group interview, I asked each woman if they could identify a specific moment when they realized they were "going to make it," through the pain they had experienced. For Rori, it wasn't about avoiding pain. It was about knowing that although pain had come, it had only come to *pass*—God wouldn't let it stay and hold her captive.

I think for me the best way I can say it is the way it came to me was when I was...You know when you're reading a fairy-tale and it says "that it came to pass." I caught on to that. And then when things start happening I would just say, 'and this too shall pass.' It came to pass. And once I accept that, it's like I can release it and move on. But as long as I'm trying [to] hold on to something, whether it's a memory, whether it's a feeling, whatever it is; it just came to pass. It's not here to stay forever. And when you realize that, you can let it go and look for the next "came to pass." Because it's all coming. But it got to pass. It can't stay here. Nothing remains the same.

Rori developed this notion of trouble that "came to pass" out of her own experience, but she recognized that her story was common. Part of her recovery from the intimate violence involved breaking the silence, and telling other girls and women how to avoid it and recover from it. While her pain in abusive relationships was very real, she worked with and through the pain and determined that she had made it through because of God.

Two particular experiences in college helped her make this determination. The first involved an encounter in church. She tried to get high before church service and had planned to hook

up for sex with a man she knew after service was over. She tried
to get high because she felt anxious, "like something's coming."
The drugs and alcohol didn't work, but she still went to church.
The message she heard changed her.

> So, I go in there, and he's preaching, and the sermon is, "Do
> you want to leave here the same way you came here?" He got
> my attention. So, that was a different Sunday for me, because I
> had planned to go home with this guy after the service. He was
> supposed to meet up, have dinner, and go have sex. It blew all
> that away, okay.
>
> My thing, my walk with God had been one that when I
> finally realized at this point right here that God was talking to
> me? And I had been listening but not listening. You know how
> you hear, but you don't listen? Okay.
>
> From that point on, I started listening, because the next day
> I had…
>
> You know [how] you call yourself a little ho'. You…you got
> an *appointment*, and you set up for your "clients." Well, my
> client was coming at Monday, so I got (pause)…and, I totally
> forgot about it. I mean, that's stuff that I just didn't do. He came
> by, and I said, oh, I'm so sorry, and I began to tell him what I
> experienced with the Lord.
>
> He left money there, and he said…I said, "What you doing
> that for?" He said, "Because if you ever backslide, I want you to
> call me." But it was like… He said, "Your conversation now is
> so different," that he knew that I was serious. I wasn't trying to
> run no scam. He said, "You're serious about this." I said, "Yeah.
> Man, it's nothing like it. It was the best thing that ever happened
> to me." So, now it's like I still believe.

Up until that transformative moment during college, Rori
hadn't taken seriously church or other spiritual phenomena she
had experienced. That moment during the sermon prompted her
to believe it really was safe to believe. Her sense that "God was
talking to me" opened her to experience a sacred acceptance,
and that in turn encouraged her to take seriously other spiritual
encounters she'd been having. For years, Rori had experienced
visitations from dying family members who would appear and
talk to her during semi-dream states of sleep just as they were

completing their transition. She had disregarded them as mere dreams without much meaning or value, that is, until the experience in church called her to consider that the dreams were a gift from God.

Her maternal grandmother had come to visit her like this a few years before she actually transitioned. During the vision she asked Rori to "take care of her baby" because she wouldn't be there much longer to do it for herself. Rori remembered the vision some time later when she got a call to come back home and take care of her critically ill mother. She left college (and the drug and alcohol abuse) behind and returned home. Rori understood the encounter in church during college and the multiple visits from transitioning family members to mean that God was interested and involved in her life. She finally felt affirmed. These two critical experiences in her spiritual journey made God real for her.

For Rori, these affirming events began an important process of building a relationship with God. With time, she gained the self-confidence to question what she had been taught in church. This questioning shed light on the hypocrisy she experienced in being raped by a church leader and simultaneously being raised to be a religious, socially conservative, Christian woman. She began re-evaluating the religious and social messages she had received about what it meant to be Black and female. In church she got the impression that women were considered weak, and she distinctly remembered how conversations about girls and women were often punctuated with the injunction that "thou shalt not." In her Church of God in Christ tradition, female bodies were something to be covered up, and sex wasn't addressed unless it was discussed within the context of marriage or in terms of how it was wrong. The onus for male sexuality was placed on the female's sexual restraint, which was interpreted as evidence of her genuine connection with the Holy Spirit. In return for upholding these sexual ideals, the message was that God would protect them and others would hold them in high spiritual regard. Conversely, girls and women who did not comply with these sexual codes were deemed lacking and unfulfilled by the Holy Spirit.

It was a turning point for Rori when she realized that obeying the sexual codes governing her sense of holiness had no real spiritual influence over her connection with God, or whether or not a man would abuse her, as she had been taught. Her healing awareness of the connection between childhood molestation, the impact of religious teachings on her identity as a woman, and the relationship choices she made were accompanied by awareness that all of this occurred within the wider context of her family's struggle to recover from multigenerational instances of abuse. Rori and her sisters were sexually assaulted, and Rori's aunt (the one whose intervention led to the end of the abuse) had also been raped by someone within the family. The struggle continued into a third generation with Rori's two sons, who were abused by their fathers. The abuse was primarily physical, but one of her sons was also incestuously molested by his birth father. During the interviews, Rori shared and reflected on her process of becoming clear about the connection between the abuse she experienced and the violence her two sons suffered:

> As an adult you think that you're past all of that. But, after I moved down here this man [Rori's childhood abuser] showed up at my door. I came down here in [date omitted]. I had already had both of my sons. As a matter of fact, I had come down here because I found out that my husband had molested my baby. I just beat my oldest son into submission, I guess. And when I found out I was like, we got to go. We can't stay here. Because if we stay here…There was so many things going on. And as a teacher I noticed it when other children were being molested. But I hadn't noticed my own. And that bothered me. Because you know, you get so caught up in your work. And I was like, work is not that important.

When Rori found out that her son was being molested, she pieced together a network of professional women and family members who helped her get herself and her sons away to a safe place. Rori shared with me that her two grandchildren, had also been abused—physically and possibly sexually—by other family members. She was proactive in doing her part to disrupt the patterns by taking a visible and vigilant role in her grandchildren's lives. As a family they have struggled with the impact of necessary legal interventions on behalf of the grand-children on the one hand and the desire to keep the family together on the other.

The force of Rori's commitment to disrupting the patterns of abuse rivaled the force of her own trauma as it re-emerged in the form of flashbacks, anxiety, and ongoing struggles with intimate connections. She developed several strategies to help her cope. Whether healthy (like singing, sewing, and breaking the silence about rape) or not (like drug and alcohol abuse), all of these strategies were directed at managing the trauma she experienced. She grounded her healing and self-recovery in the strength she gained from her faith, relationships with other women, truth-telling about sexual violence in her family and the community, and active involvement in her church's music ministry.

Eliza

"Oh, Yeah, I'm Still Here in God's Grace…God's Grace"

When Eliza came to the table, she sat down like a woman who had looked back over her life and was now retelling it from a vantage point that spoke to the meaning she had made of her pain. When we talked one-on-one, as well as when she spoke during the group sessions, she shared how difficult some parts of this process were for her. Part of the difficulty was simply an aspect of talking about pain. Another part was that these conversations were a first for her. Up until the interviews, she had shared publicly bits and pieces of what had happened to her. But, this was the first time she had ever pulled the violent incidents in her life together to speak about them in a cohesive narrative. When it was her turn to share with the group, she waited until she had everyone's attention at the table, and began to read the manuscript she brought with her.

> How have I dealt with my hurts and my anger and my losses and my pain? I write about it, about them. Some of them I dissolve in the memory bank of my hurts. Some of them I forget for a long time in order not to allow them to continue to hurt me. My first

book [name omitted] was published in [date omitted] because two brothers read the pieces and felt they were for all people. The [name of book omitted] are from the journals I kept over the years, and from them took pieces and made into a book of poems or expressions. Later on I came to realize that as a sexually abused child I was acting out my belief that sex (intercourse) meant love, was love, or at least meant "I love you." I'm the firstborn child of 10 children, 5 boys and 5 girls. As a firstborn, I guess I was then given the job of performing fellatio on my father to assist him when he suffered with migraine headaches. Apparently, my sucking on his penis helped relieve the pain he had in his head. [Eliza laughs]

And, you know, it was all I could do. I was trying to be straight with this because you know I wanted to say my sucking on one head helped the pain in his other head. Well, I did anyway.

As a sexually abused child I did not know that love was not intercourse.

Eliza was grown before it became clear to her that what happened between her and her father was abuse. Moving into her grandmother's house saved her. It took her out of her abusive father's incestuous reach, and it gave her ties with a mother figure who nurtured her in ways that her birth mother had not. It was a safer, and far more affirming environment than her own home. Yet despite the move, she continued to experience abuse. The next time the abuser was a stranger in her new neighborhood who violated her out in public:

Eliza: But, it was all in the atmosphere because even down in the commission houses. You know the commission houses are where the trains are that come in with the vegetables and things and little girls wear underpants that have elastic. No, they didn't have elastic, they just had a lot of little bands around their panties and the bums would be watching. We would play jacks and we'd be squatting down there and...

Stephanie: And they would be looking in between your legs?

Eliza: Yeah. And we were aware of this. I remember one man, I was coming home from some place and he said, you show me yours and I'll show you mine. And he said, "For 50 cents..."

And you know, I remember going back there for the 50 cents.
I don't remember seeing nothing (chuckling). But, I don't
remember buying the two Hostess cupcakes I love and I was
going to get to get [sic]. Yeah, you know. It makes me feel all
sad (crying).
Stephanie: It is sad. It is very sad. That's very sad.
Eliza: Oh, somebody...And I think that's why you know,
when I talk about sex, you know...Really we carry so much
crap. And we carry so much shame about what we've *had* to
do...to do what we do (crying).

Eliza shared this part of her story apart from the rest of the
group when we met one-on-one. It was a hard moment for us
both. It was hard for her to tell, and her pain and sadness were
hard for me to witness.

Eliza also experienced violence in her adult relationships. She
began the conversation about her adult encounters by recount-
ing a fairly recent incident of being hit in the face by a long-time
friend with whom she'd become romantically involved. She was
shocked and amazed when it happened. She considered him a
friend, so his violence was particularly unexpected. It reminded
her of the time when her jealous ex-husband strangled her during a family trip. She remembered the horror and how important it was to stay quiet while he nearly choked her to death in
the hallway of their friend's home because she didn't want the
children to wake up and see what was happening.

Even when she was experiencing violence, Eliza always tried
to put her children first. She vividly recalled a moment when
her efforts to keep her children safe were deeply misunderstood
by her daughter. During one of her marriages, she realized that
her husband had set his eyes on her daughters. At the time, she
and her younger children had been living out of the country on
a military base with her husband who was a serviceman and
fifteen years her junior. The recollection of his taunting confession of how he had made sexual advances toward her daughter
brought her to tears.

Eliza: I was having this toe surgery and when we were in [name
of country omitted]...And he came to the hospital to tell me
that he had asked [daughter's name omitted] to lay in bed

with him. Well, now you know, I went into overkill. I was like "oh, let me get my child out of here." And you know how she interpreted it? That I choose him. I'm like...I sent her to [name of state omitted] to my daughter.

Stephanie: Oh, you were trying to get her out of the house as opposed to sending him away?

Eliza: Yes, yes. 'Cause he's military. We're in [name of foreign country omitted].

Stephanie: Oh. Oh. On base?

Eliza: Yes. I have to get a hop to get out of there. So honey, I don't even know where the money came from. Well, you can fly out in a cargo plane, sitting on the side, like you're luggage.

Stephanie: How dumb?

Eliza: Yeah.

Stephanie: So you sent her away to get her out of the house?

Eliza: (Nodding) I sent her to [name of state omitted] to family...to family.

Stephanie: To get her out of the house.

Eliza's daughter interpreted her mother's actions to mean that she had chosen her husband over her own child. Another of Eliza's daughters also reported being approached by their stepfather. This daughter told her that he "said things" to her, but to this day Eliza doesn't know what was said. She and this daughter are estranged from one another. Eliza didn't talk much at all about her sons and she continued to struggle with sadness over ups and downs with her children. Her reflection on how her choices impacted her and her children reveal the complex nature of her struggle. First, she was struggling with her own psychological trauma from being sexually assaulted in childhood and battered as an adult woman. She also carried the weight of concern over how she looked and measured up to social standards as a divorced, unmarried Black woman mothering five children by different fathers. This additional social pressure compounded the effects of the violence, in that she also felt judged and stigmatized:

I had five children. *I had no man living there, okay!* Except when I was married and then, you know he was working fortunately, but those didn't last long. And then I married the 15 year younger one the second time and uh, so that was, you know, like bringing a wolf in the house.

As an African American woman coming of age in the socially conservative fifties and sixties, she took pride in the fact that she never lived with a man who wasn't her husband. It was a way to lay claim to and honor herself as a mother in spite of how others may have judged her. Even with her self-determination to honor the mother that she was, she still felt tension over the painful consequences of her intimate decisions, a tension compounded by social expectations of what constituted good mothering.

There have been seasons of strife and reconciliation in the relationships Eliza has with her children and other family members. Within the year or so leading up to her participation in the research for this book, she had gone public with the news that she was HIV positive. Of all the responses, the most painful one came from a family member who judged and rejected her for being infected with the virus. This was a deeply disappointing moment for Eliza. She had hoped to receive compassion from this relative, but that was not the case. On the other hand, the most positive and embracing responses came from her church community, which had proved to be a safe space for her in various seasons of her life. For example, when she was incestuously assaulted as a child by her father, her grandmother took her in and kept her actively engaged in the life of the church she pastored. Years later, the church provided another safe space for her when her more recent congregation embraced her leadership on breaking silences around HIV/AIDS and Black sexuality.

Her ministry emerged out of her journey of sexual and spiritual discovery. Whereas at one time sex was a coping strategy that helped Eliza soothe the symptoms of violence that began when she was very young, she later replaced that strategy by writing about sex, relationships, desire, pain, hope, and God. Her poetry was based on journals she wrote over the years. She also wrote about skin color, race and racism, spirituality, and justice. Writing, reading, and speaking about where she has been, the seasons she has traveled, and the self-acceptance she found in God's love helped her "deal" with the complexities of her journey:

> I just really write my stuff...See, I was brown. I was too dark to be in that group, yes, yes. And then my parents were not doctors, school principals, or teachers, all right? So I was the little brown, dark child, poor dark child, raised by my grandmother. And, you know, parents split up, Mama in the kitchen telling me to get the butcher knife so she can cut my stepfather, interesting things like that. So, you know, I was in that craziness for a while. So that's what I write about.

Writing is where Eliza worked out her traumatic experiences, and much of working it out had to do with the gratification she felt in being able to help someone by letting them know that they were not alone. In short, she rarely shared her story simply for the purposes of her own healing. That was secondary to her primary concern to help others. When I asked her about when and how she chose to tell her story, it occurred to her that she had not ever intentionally done so for her own healing and recovery.

> *Eliza*: ...Um, when you talk about having a space, a place, that is just my space, my time? That might be scary. Maybe that's why. It could be. That means I have to trust you. Cause see, I be *evaluating* stuff. You know, I do. (chuckling)
>
> *Stephanie*: Only a fool enters therapy without thinking about who it is that they're going to be working with. It's a very wise, self-loving thing to do.
>
> *Eliza*: Yeah.
>
> *Stephanie*: To be, um, concerned.
>
> *Eliza*: Yeah. So, I don't know. I don't know. Plus, then there is...It's like, "time for myself?" Oh wow. What a new concept! Am I ready for that at 80? Oh goodness.
>
> Oh, you know...Maybe I should? [But] shouldn't I be writing something or reading something or over at Bible study at church, or, you know, be down at the school?
>
> *Stephanie*: The idea of doing it for yourself is a little scary?
>
> *Eliza*: Hmm, very different.
>
> *Stephanie*: Um–hum. Um–hum. It would be. It would be.
>
> *Eliza*: Yeah, yeah.

Although Eliza did not choose to seek out the kind of space that would intentionally focus on her healing, she did find healing in her vocation as a writer and teacher, and in active participation in her church. Her favorite classroom moments were opportunities in which she participated in the liberation of her seminary students who struggled with shame from sexual violence and physical assault. Work in the church, classroom, and community was incredibly affirming, and these spaces provided her with the kind of contact that supported her self-recovery and healing. In each of these spaces, she found multiple ways to share what she found to be most important in her life—love for and from God and freedom in her life because of that love.

Cirene

"Black People Don't Need to Go See Therapy. We Got the Church. We Got God"

I noticed Cirene's quiet demeanor as she made her way to the table where the group had gathered to meet and talk for the first time. She was intentional about her reasons for coming. She said that sharing her story was a way for her to "take back her power" from the older member of her extended family who repeatedly molested and raped her:

I've never been a very...(I wrote something, but I'll just say it) I remember [being] in the midst of a very extended family. My mother is from [name of city omitted]. So in 1950, her [sic] and her parents, they migrated to [name of city omitted] and they bought a house and an apartment building. So I grew up around cousins, my grandparents, my grand aunties. I mean, everywhere I turned around it was just family...family...family. So, a very trusting family. Christian family. Always in the church. Always involved in missionary work and stuff like that. And so my grandmom's son—my grandmom [name omitted], actually—who was my second cousin, [name of cousin omitted]; he molested me when I was eight years old. And so I just remember my first oral sex experience was with him. I remember him always touching me, grabbing me. I don't remember if there was exact penetration. But, I just remember the experience just really hurt. I remember he used to put lotion on his penis like a lubrication. And he used to clean me every time before he did anything with me. All the time. So I guess I was having yeast infections or some type of infections because he was always up in me. And, so from then I just remember feeling like really depressed and being an angry child growing up. I'd always just have attitude. Always getting into it with my father. Very emotional. Always crying. I remember my dad used to say, "Stop all the crying. Stop all the crying."

So for years, once I stopped crying, it took me a long, long, long, long time, even when I was in seminary, to really start to regain my emotions and really start to cry again. And I remember I suppressed the memory. And I remember being in high school and I was just sitting at my dining room table. And I was like, "I was molested." And it just hit me really, really hard. I remember calling my friend, my best friend. And I was like, "[name omitted], I just remember being molested when I was a child." And she was young. We were both young. She was like, "Oh, so was he cute?" I was like, what does that have to do with anything? And I was just like, okay, you're not the person that I need to talk to about this, obviously. And so, I remember going and transitioning from [name omitted] High School into [name omitted] High School.

And I remember going to my mom. I was like…mom, I'm just really depressed. I just really need somebody to talk to. I need to go see a therapist. She was like, "Black people don't need to go see therapy. We got the church. We got God; so, no." I was like, okay, this is not going to work. So, I remember doing some research on campus and finding out that [name of school] offers free therapy. So, I remember checking myself into therapy. And a couple months later my mom was like what's wrong with you? She was like, "I see this change, this transformation in you." And I was like, well, I've been seeing a therapist behind your back. And she was just so glad. She was like I'm so glad you went against my better judgment. I'm so glad that you have wisdom enough in yourself that you needed to see somebody. And she was like, "Can I go to therapy sessions with you?" It went from "You don't need to see anybody" to "Let me go with you." And I remember as soon as I started to speak about my cousin…(He went away for years…I didn't see him. He was starting high school. He molested me. I was eight years old. He

was like 16 or 17.) And as soon as I started talking to my therapist about it...I remember it being Christmas break and I had
enough courage to tell my mom.

It probably was a couple days later or maybe a week at the
max; he shows up at my house. And I'm like, oh my gosh. So, I
open the door and he's there. And I remember mom was upstairs
in her room. And I went upstairs. And I was like, mom, [name
omitted] is downstairs. I was like, don't trip. Don't say nothing.
Let me handle this. And this expression on her face was like,
"I'm going to say something." I'm like, Momma please, I'm not
ready for this. I'm really not ready for this. Just don't say anything. And so, I really thought...They was in there talking or
whatever, and I was in the den. I heard the door close. (Yay. She
didn't say anything.) All of the sudden I heard, "Cirene, come
to the front room." I was like, 'shit.' And so, she was there and
[name omitted] was there. And he was sitting down in this posture of like, "Oh my God. I've just been caught." She was like,
"So, Cirene, what do you have to say? He said he didn't do it."
I was like, well...(I mean, she believed me and all). I was like,
"Mom, what do you expect him to say?" Of course, he's going
to deny it or whatever.

And so, after the incident we had this discussion. She went
back upstairs, and I went to the kitchen and I took a knife, and
I just started cutting myself. And that was the start of me, kind
of, self-mutilation. And, I just started cutting myself from then
on. I remember going to school, living in the dorms. It wouldn't
happen all the time, but just big emotional bursts that I really
couldn't handle, I just started taking knives or whatever I could
find and just started cutting on my arms.

Cirene started cutting (self-mutilating) when she was a teenager. She would cut herself when she remembered the rape,
became angry, or felt threatened. She was angry about being
incestuously raped, but she was also angry over being rendered
emotionally mute when her father (unaware of what had happened to her) told her to 'stop all that crying' about an offense that
she had every right to lament. It was years later before she found
support that helped her claim that right. Until then, though, her
struggles with the consequences of rape and emotional silence
manifested in cutting, depression, and panic attacks throughout

her teen and college years. The depression prompted her therapist to suggest that she consider psychiatric medication:

> My psychologist wanted to put me on some medicine which she
> recommended—I think some antidepressants and stuff like that.
> And even when I was younger, I really had anxiety problems—
> panic attacks. I know the doctors wanted to put me on medica-
> tion, but my grandmother wouldn't let me—wouldn't let them.
> And so anxiety and panic are something that I have been work-
> ing with or dealing with ever since I was a young child.

The conversation about whether or not she would take psychiatric medication began in adolescence. That conversation
resurfaced in college as she continued to struggle with a painful
past that continued to affect her. Cirene acted out, cut herself,
and used the popular club drug Ecstasy to help her manage the
intense symptoms of sexual trauma, depression and anxiety.
These coping behaviors were part of the strategies she developed to maintain herself, but there were also others. One strategy involved finding images, narratives, and relationships that
featured women in positions of power.

These women were ideals who embodied the kind of presence and power that she felt had been taken from her when her
cousin raped her. Her search began in middle and junior high
school with the Black, all girl, hip-hop group, TLC. She, her sister, and another friend would come home after school and dress
up like members of the group. Cirene would play Left Eye, the
notoriously sexual "bad girl" of the crew. This play time opened
up a space for her to take on a role that was very different for
her. Sexual, loud, and brash, Left Eye offered an idea of what it
would look like to posture in ways that were very different from
the obedient good-girl image she portrayed in school. It also
allowed her to express her sexuality in a safe space—a space
of play and imagination that was very much different from the
sexual violation she experienced in incest:

> *Cirene*: And like for me being like Left Eye, she was, like, the
> cool-ass bad chick, you know?
> *Stephanie*: Um–hum.

Cirene: And so that, that was really cool to me to kind of—because throughout school, I was like, very passive, very quiet, very submissive, always wanted to be like, a good girl. I even remember one time in class...

Like, you know, when we had to go to the bathroom, we got out the red slip...And this little corner [was like red, and] "red be bad." And I remember I didn't raise my hand. And so, I'd sat there and I peed on myself. Because I didn't want to raise my hand. I was like, oh my God; I can't be associated with this red slip. And so, I mean, that's how quiet and very passive I was, but at home, it was a different story. So it was very cool to find a type of power through Left Eye and through like, the girl kind of group power of TLC.

At school Cirene didn't want to do anything to draw attention to herself. But, dressing up like Left Eye outside of school allowed her to be seen in a different light. This character was one among several female heroines like pop-rock musician Alanis Morissette, who played significant roles in Cirene's journey. Morissette's voice sounded an alarm, and Cirene received her voice as permission to unmute her own pain:

Cirene: Just her music like, Hand In My Pocket, Ironic and Utopia. Like, I remember getting all her CDs and stuff like that. Just to really listen to her and just like...the way she just expressed herself...And so, I found like...I just really, really...I liked it. One, because, you know, for a Black chick to listen to rock music, I went to a white school, so that's how it came on that end. But, at home, my dad...He said, "Why are you listening to this music?" This and that. And so, it was cool kind of, to do something different. But I really kind of liked her rage and as she progressed in her music, she kind of found this peace within herself.

Stephanie: Alanis?

Cirene: (Nodding) Alanis Morissette. And so I just—I really just found myself really getting lost in her music and I remember just yelling aloud and I remember kind of identifying with like, the screams where she express[ed] herself in music.

Cirene didn't just listen to and watch performers like Left Eye and Morissette. She participated in their art; it became an avenue that allowed her to express and explore parts of her inner world that had been silenced, forbidden, and shamed. Even if it meant connecting vicariously, these musical heroines met her very real need to connect with empowering female ideas and images. The idealization of female pop-culture heroines and her fantasy attachments with these women were critical. Going deep into these characters was an important alternative to other coping behaviors she used to fend off the disempowerment she felt from being raped. These female heroines also met the need to address the gap she felt in her relationship with her mother.

Cirene had a close relationship with her mother, but her mother's preoccupation with maintaining her family's reputation and standing in their community often overshadowed this intimacy. This was difficult in general for Cirene, but the difficulty was further complicated by another silence that she was trying to break around her emerging identity and sexual attraction to females. While her mother was willing to hear Cirene about what was going on with her, this willingness was matched by the equal, and at times overriding, concern about how the community might judge the family. This was a constant point of tension for Cirene as she navigated her developing lesbian identity:

> *Cirene*: I come from a family that's all—especially when my grandparents were still alive—it was all about perception. About, "You're a [family name omitted], you gotta act this way, you gotta do that, you gotta do this"—and I hated it. I hated being so closed-in and self-censoring. It was just too much. I'm like, "Why I gotta take all this pressure 'cause I was born in this family?" And I feel that I couldn't express myself the way that I wanted to in the open, so I did it behind closed doors. And I remember I got all piercings and stuff, and I wanted to always have my face, my eyebrows pierced, my nose pierced. I wanted a hoop in my lip, and I told myself I couldn't do it because I was a leader in church, and as a young child I can't get up there with all these piercings in my face because people wouldn't take me seriously. So I just got my

> body pierced. I got my vagina pierced, I got my belly button
> pierced, I had all my ears pierced, had my tongue pierced.
> *Stephanie*: Wait a minute—you had...
> *Cirene*: Yeah, I got my clit pierced. I did. I did.
> *Stephanie*: Didn't that hurt?
> *Cirene*: It was just a pinch, I mean, but it was just something
> about it—something about saying I wanted to do something
> that was just so out the box and actually doing it—it was
> such a rush.

Even though Cirene and her mother were able to talk, her
mother was slow to accept her lesbian identity. This was a
stumbling block in Cirene's connection with her mother, and
as she grew older, it became the underlying impetus for Cirene
to seek out connections with other women (mentors, therapists, other women in the community) who could embrace her
fully.

One of the most influential women was her female therapist
in college, the one mentioned earlier, who helped her develop
the courage to reveal that she had been raped by a family member. Cirene pursued other healing relationships with women,
including one that led her back to church where she eventually worked through the tension between her reality and her
family's public expectations. She began counseling with a Black
female Christian counselor and was positively influenced by a
female pastor in her local congregation. In that congregation
she worked through shame over having been raped, and ultimately began to recognize that God had called her to ministry.
The congregation was very comforting and encouraging about
healing from the abuse, but it was far less accepting when they
found out she was same-gender loving.

The tension that Cirene faced in these important relationships existed against the backdrop of a spiritual journey that
led her beyond Christianity. In college she studied religion and
exposed herself to various faith traditions, including Buddhism,
which she found extremely helpful in dealing with an underlying sense of shame and rejection. Counseling, Buddhism, church
and her educational journey provided experiences that affirmed
the multiple dimensions of Cirene's identity: African American,

woman, Spiritual, and woman-loving. These experiences were critical in healing the violence and trauma symptoms that began when she was a child. Cirene's journey of self-recovery led her to a vocation in Christian ministry with same-gender loving women and women who have experienced sexual abuse.

Tamara

"…Had I Not Believed in God, I Would Have Been Done"

With a wide smile and bright brown eyes, Tamara introduced herself to the group as an artist. She literally opened her mouth and sang her introduction. She came because she wanted to talk about the role that art played in her journey to heal from being molested by an older cousin. She told us that many years had passed after the abuse before the memories became clear enough for her to recognize that what had been done to her was incest:

I woke up one morning and I could hear momma and my aunt [name omitted] in there talking in the middle room of the house. And I remember getting up and going in. I was still kind of sleepy. And they were talking. And I liked to hear the sound of their voices, but I kept yawning. Mommy told me to go back to bed ("I don't want to go"), and I was kind of whiny. So, there were two bunk beds in the room. And the boys were in the bunk beds in the same room. So, Aunt [name omitted] said, "Well, just go get in the bed." [Name omitted] was in the middle bed. So, I liked to climb. So, I climbed in the middle bed. I remember just lying there. And I was about to drift back off to sleep and I remembered him taking my hand. And he stuck it through the fly on his boxers, on his pajamas. I remember him rubbing my hand up and down the shaft of his penis. It was odd. It was just very strange. But, I didn't say anything. I mean, everybody was in the room. And I didn't say anything. And he kept rubbing my hand up and down the shaft of his penis. And I'm trying to figure out what's going on because I've never seen one of these things. I don't know what I'm touching. There are no men in my house. I don't know what's going on. All of the sudden he jumps out of the bed and he runs to the bathroom.

And I remember my aunt, although...All the women were laughing because they thought he had to go to the bathroom really bad and that he had waited a long time. And so later that day, I think I was supposed to go get somebody some water. And I had gone to the kitchen and I was coming back with the water. I can't remember why, but I remember coming through the living room on my way back to where the women were. And [name omitted] was there. And he asked me did I want to play. And I wanted to play. So I remember him pulling down my brown corduroy pants (because they were my favorite pants). I remember him pulling them down and bending me over the couch. And I don't remember whether he tried any penetration or not. But, I do remember him rubbing his penis up and down my butt. And all of the sudden he, again...I heard someone coming. I think Momma called my name or something. Anyway, he left me bent over the couch and he just slammed out of the front door. Ran out of the house. And I didn't know what was going on but I knew something bad was happening. So I remember I ran into the closet and I started fixing my clothes. And my mother was calling me. I guess she heard me in the closet. She opened the door. She saw me trying to fix my pants. And she said, "What happened?" She was kind of stern or fussing? I don't know.

It scared me and I started crying. So, she pulled me to the couch and she said, "What happened?" And so I started telling her. And so she took me to my grandmother and she started yelling for [name omitted]. She said, "Where is he? Where is he?" And he had run outside. I had a pony. And he had run outside to where the horses were. And [name omitted] said he just flew out of here and went down there. Anyway, they called him back in. I remember by this time I was sitting with my grandmother in her bed. I had a bowl of ice cream. My aunt [name omitted] was crying. And my mother told [name omitted], she confronted him about what happened. And she told him that he was not welcome in our home anymore.

Tamara was three years old when her older cousin molested her. It was many years later, when she was in college and working at a shelter for battered teenage girls, that the fuzzy edges around these memories sharpened and the molestation came into focus. The clarity came when one of the workers at the shelter asked her outright, "Are you an incest survivor?" She was taken aback by the question, and was even more thrown off when the woman told her that she had the "mannerisms of a survivor." Tamara didn't recall what she said or had been doing that prompted the woman's observations, but when the shock wore off she responded, "I am...I am...." The suppressed memories had been there all along. An alienating sense of shame came along with the clarity that an older cousin had molested her and it created a tension between who she had previously known herself to be, and the image of herself that was taking shape in light of this new awareness. These feelings were exacerbated and perhaps compounded by the grief she felt over the loss and absence of connections with male family members; some of which had been severed after the molestation, and others that had been lost much earlier.

Although her mother had several sisters and brothers, Tamara described a general sense of being isolated from males in the family, including her mother's brothers. It was unclear to Tamara whether or not her mother kept her away from them to protect her from being violated, but it was evident that her mother was very concerned about having males around her daughter. During the interviews Tamara recalled as a young child asking her mother why she didn't date. In all of her years Tamara couldn't recall ever seeing her mother bring a male love interest into their home. "Your father would love you, and he was so excited about you coming. And I cannot promise that any man would love you the way he did, and I'm not willing to take that chance." Tamara's father died while her mother was pregnant. After her father's death, her mother relocated and moved back in with Tamara's grandmother. Tamara experienced her mother's concern as overprotection and it deepened her yearning for significant connections with males in general, and father figures in particular. Although Tamara never had the chance to meet him, her father's absence was a presence in and of itself. This yearning for significant male connections also showed up in the complex way that she described her relationship with God.

For her, God was a surrogate father who was present and available to her. This relationship was complex because although

she experienced love and connection with God as her heav-
enly father, she also experienced an intensely painful distance
at times. She felt a close connection with God during periods
of time when she abstained from sex, but this intimacy was
matched by an equally powerful sense of shame and distance
when she was sexually active.

Part of the shame was related to being incestuously molested,
but another part of it was external. During the third round of
interviews that specifically focused on sex and sexuality, Tamara
wept when she talked about adults in her church who publicly
shamed her when they found out that she was sexually active.
She was a teenager at the time. Though that was decades ago,
her tears let us know that the pain was still very fresh to her.
Members of the congregation brought her before the church to
confess her sexual sins, and then make a public apology. She
refused to do it and especially remembered feeling singled out
from other teens in the community. Others had been sexually
active, but Tamara recalled feeling like she was the only one who
had been forced to confess that she had sinned by having sex.
For her, it was the community's way of putting her in her place.
This sense of being targeted and then isolated as an outsider followed her through adolescence and even into adulthood. While
those feelings initially showed up only around dating and sex,
as she got older, they also pervaded other areas of her life.

Tamara was a classically trained opera singer. Her appreciation for the arts began with her mother requiring that she take
dance and music classes when she was young. She enjoyed the
classes because they made her feel good, but she also felt like the
classes invited criticism from community members who believed
that her interest in art suggested that she thought she was better
than other Black people in the community:

But, I think what saved me, even if I didn't know I needed saving, was the fact that I became a performing artist. So I was
always doing the art myself. Like, my mother was one for lessons. I had piano lessons and I had dance lessons and I had
singing lessons and I think she thought I was gonna grow out of
that, but I never did. So she's like, "Okay, we could have skipped

that one." But, you know, I just did that all the time. And...But, it was opera. So, it was a little weird because for a long time even though I loved it, I felt very alienated from Black people because I'm in a—I'm from a very small, small town. We lived 20 miles from the nearest town and we're small enough that when I was growing up the nearest movie theater was 100 miles one way. So yeah, we were real tight knit there. And so it was very—it was something—it was an ostracizing thing, my art was an ostracizing thing even though I was in the show choir and I've always felt—I've always been on the outside looking in.

When I got to college I did a recital in February, and this was part of the narrative during my recital: "I went to college and I was so excited because I would be singing opera and everybody would be there singing opera and we'd all be doing it and I wouldn't be weird." But, I found other weirdness to be associated with. I mean, you were still Black in a white school, you were still female in a place that was, you know, predominantly male, it was still some outsiderness in the art form.

Although being a young Black woman opera singer made her feel like an outsider, she clung to what spoke to her. During her first semester she met African American opera singer, Kathleen Battle. Kathleen's voice and physical presence on stage made an indelible impact on Tamara.

It was just this light ethereal sound and she was just singing and it was amazing, and it was my first live operatic experience and I was like, "Wow, that Black woman is doing the damn thing." She was doing it. And I was like, I want to do *that*. And I went to meet her and she was just so tiny and rude and tiny (laughing). She was rude. At least I thought it was rude, I understand now what she was doing, but she is rude. But, you know, it was something that I had started—I wanted to do. I wanted to do it before, but I saw it being done and I was like, "Okay, I can do this now. I want to do *this*."

She began researching opera singers and discovered Black vocalists and composers who hadn't been written into the mainstream music histories offered in her music classes. Being rooted in this under-told history gave her a sense of racial pride, but it also engendered a sense of alienation as one of very few African Americans pursuing opera. As she pursued classic vocal training, she also sought out cultural activities that connected her to African cultural traditions, which ultimately played a significant role in her spiritual growth. During college she enrolled in African dance classes instructed by two women who taught dances practiced by devotees of Voudou and Santeria, diasporic derivatives of African tradition religions. This was critical because this non-Christian context helped her tap into her spiritual gifts, which she interpreted as a sign that God accepted her and had a plan for her life, regardless of what faith tradition she pursued, or what sense of alienation she experienced.

Dance helped Tamara develop a relationship with God beyond and aside from the beliefs that were handed to her in childhood by her mother, grandmother, and church community. She was raised in the Baptist tradition, but this non-Christian experience was an important time of spiritual awakening for her. Dance was part of a developmental moment in which she came into the awareness that she had the spiritual gift of prophecy. Her understanding was that this prophetic capacity came from God and that it called her to be a truthteller. This was significant because being endowed with a gift from God empowered her to combat the sense of shame and alienation she felt in her relationship with God. The challenge, though, was that even though she felt as if the gift was God's way of embracing her, she struggled deeply with accepting the grace that came with it.

Inasmuch as Tamara felt called to speak truth about wrongdoing, she feared that same scrutiny by others would expose the "dirt" in her own life. She approached various spiritual teachers to develop clarity about her prophetic voice and calling to discipleship, but her shame and fear often prevented her from walking in this ministry. And yet, despite this, she believed that God indeed gave her the words to speak the truth, and this strengthened her when she struggled to believe God's grace. There were seasons in her life when being an artist counteracted the shame and alienation that had been a part of her narrative since childhood. But there were also others moments when criticism from others who didn't accept the pleasure she experienced in opera influenced her away from the art. After years of staying away, she resumed her career. This was significant for Tamara. She found great joy in performances that once again opened up her creativity, empowered her to reconnect with God, and prompted her to embrace her spiritual gifts (and herself) more fully.

Octavia

"I'm Still Here, You Know? I Do Have Some Worth..."

Octavia is cinnamon-colored, with a warm and somewhat quiet demeanor. Unlike the others in the group who first experienced violence as girls, she was an adult when she was assaulted. She was brutally raped and beaten by strangers in a hotel room. When she talked with me to consider participating in the research study, she was emphatic about her reason for participating. Sharing her testimony was an opportunity to wipe her hands clean, and drop the emotional weight of rape:

A little over 20 years ago I was on a date with a man who I had dated previously for several years. This date was an attempt to reconcile and give the relationship another shot (because I still loved him and he was unfaithful and started seeing someone else). And we went through the whole, "please forgive me" and "I've got to do better," etcetera, etcetera. So, we went to [name of restaurant omitted]. And you could say he wined me and dined me. Unfortunately, I became weak and agreed to go to a nice motel with him in [name of city omitted]...When we got to the hotel, the hotel attendant put us in a room around the side of the motel where there were no cars. So, it was just us. We were the only ones in there on that side of the motel. And after a while there was a knock at the door. And someone was motioning with a towel. And we didn't call and ask for any towels. So, I told—I'll just call him "Bo," not his real name. I said don't answer because we didn't ask for any towels. I guess curiosity just prompted him to open the door. And he opened it with the chain on the door. But, they stuck in a shot gun and forced the door open. It was three of them. And I was naked. They said give us all your money and your jewelry, etcetera. And they said, "we're going to take your car" and do whatever.

And I was naked. So, that was, I guess, a little bit too much for them. They had to just follow through with whatever they usually think of. And, so I was sexually assaulted and sodomized. And Bo was shot in the head. Because after they took me in the bathroom and did what they were going to do, and then came out of the bathroom to do it again. And they were holding a gun on Bo. And he couldn't see what they were doing but he knew he had to do something. It was like, look, they're probably going to kill us anyway. So, he just kind of rushed for the guy with the gun. And that made me get up and start hitting the guys. They were punching me. I was punching them.

But, luckily, one of them just ran out the door. Another one, before he ran out the door, he shot Bo in the head. So, he's alive. He's okay. Luckily he didn't die.

Octavia vividly remembered that when she finally got home from the hospital, all she wanted to do was take a shower. She talked about taking a bar of soap into her mouth to clean away the terror she had just experienced. She said she felt like damaged goods and washing became a ritual that she repeated for a long time to try to flush away the trauma. She also remembered her silence about what happened. Although her mother and grandmother knew something was wrong, it was a while before she told them (or anyone else) what happened that night.

Alone, she struggled with the overwhelming pain. She grieved what had been done to her, the memory of seeing a man she loved shot in the head, the loss of their relationship, the loss of safety she now felt, and how the assault affected how she felt about herself. Albeit painstakingly slow, she moved through this particular phase of her grief and pain by listening to jazz music:

So, when I went through this and he [Bo] couldn't really be there for me...Because I was afraid. Just afraid all the time and needed to be safe. And when I didn't get it, I said...Well...I felt very alone. I felt very alone even though I had family. It was still like there was this...It was like everybody was on the outside.

And I really took refuge in Sade and then...[Octavia makes a gesture of feeling low and the group laughs].

I mean, I just wanted to just *wallow* in that sadness. I mean, to me it was just, you know, her music was so where I was, you know? I said, "Wow, I wonder if she went through this?" You know? And, "I wonder if...I wonder how she feels?" I just really wonder how she feels. So, I just kept listening and listening and listening and it seems like the more that I listened, you know, the really the sadder I became, you know?

The music...It's all the way *down*. And I think because, you know, it was in my car, and it was in my house. I was living with my mother at the time and she was like, "You know, that music is really too much." And I would cry, too. I would just—as soon as I would put in the tape, because it was a tape then...But you know what, sometimes when you're at that point you want to be sad, you know? You want to be sad. I'm not sure why, but I needed to just process through that.

At one point Octavia's mother suggested that she begin counseling with the (male) pastor of their local Baptist church to get help with the depression. While she knew that the pastor was trying to be helpful, she felt as if he was trying to "hypnotize" her into forgetting what happened. It didn't work. She could still hear and feel Sade's melancholy voice as it veiled painful memories of sodomy and a brutal physical assault. What she did find helpful during this time was continued contact with other Black women, especially the ones in her church. She recalled the breakthrough moment when her grief began to shift:

But, finally it was one day...I was...and that's why I love this book you know [pointing to a copy of Iyanla Vanzant's book, *One Day My Soul Just Opened Up*]. Because one day my soul *did* just open up and I was in church and I was listening to, you know, "I Love to Praise Him." And it was just something (and it was the pastor's daughter who was singing it, too). And it was just something about the way she sang that song, you know? And it's like she could block out all that sadness and it was like...And I just kept thinking about, you know, "I'm still here." You know? "I do have some worth, I do have some worth." Because, of course, I felt, you know, very much worthless. And

I said, you know, I'm gonna join the choir. I'm gonna join the choir. And everybody kind of knew what had happened to me and I tell you, those women, they just did just like this [wrapping her arms around herself], you know? They just did just like this [hugging herself]...

And, you know, we would go out and we would...You know, I come from—it wasn't a really small church but I grew up in that church, I was baptized there. And we would go out and sing at different churches and different places. And I just cannot tell you how that healed me, you know? Just singing and really believe in the words that I was singing. And that's why sometimes even at rehearsal, you know, I have to really just hold on to myself because, you know, you start thinking about [what] you've gone through and I think about that circle of women that really just— they just would not let me slip and fall back into that Sade thing.

The "Sade thing" made room for Octavia's grief, but she needed something more than just a space that could tolerate her grief. She needed voices of hope, and she found that in connections with other Black women in her church, as well as in Black women writers. Reading Iyanla Vanzant and Susan L. Taylor, who are both well known among African American women for their spiritual insight on Black women's lives, was salvific for Octavia. She brought excerpts from Vanzant's *One Day My Soul Just Opened Up*[2] and Taylor's *In the Spirit*[3] to share with the group during the second gathering. When she read them, it was as if she *encountered* them as wisdombearers who spoke truth in ways that gave her life. Studying Taylor and Vanzant's musings about Black women's inner lives helped Octavia ground herself in hope, but she also decided to pursue further healing through counseling for help with symptoms of PTSD and other concerns that had begun to surface. She was in individual therapy for two years and spent about a year in group therapy. Part of her healing focused heavily on the beliefs she developed about the maleness of God and what that maleness meant for her identity, spirituality, and beliefs about men following a brutal attack by men.

This was important because at one point she took the attack as evidence that she had missed the mark in her relationship with God. This theological interpretation of the violence she suffered added guilt and self-blame to the shame, fear, and loss she felt about the attack and her relationship with the man she was dating. She began working through this in therapy, but she also found help in dialogue with people from religious traditions outside of Protestantism (Catholicism, Buddhism, African traditional religions) who helped her flesh out the reasoning within her beliefs. The clearer she became about the voice of God, and finding God in herself, the more she began to also examine the role that Jesus played in her life. She realized that the male imagery and language she used to speak of God trickled down into her beliefs about Jesus. In fact, she had cast Jesus as a surrogate male presence who fulfilled her needs for protection and intimate companionship when she felt unsafe and unwanted by men following the attack. "I'll just use myself at that time. If you don't have a man, right? Or, if the man you did have, you no longer have, you tend to replace Jesus with that need...to have that void filled."

The maleness of Jesus became a significant part of Octavia's healing. She felt intimately connected with the historical figure who is at the heart of the Christian faith, and this connection brought with it a sense of physical, sexual, and emotional safety; feeling honored, and acceptance. In the wake of a brutal attack, Jesus became the man who was all of the things that men had not been to her. Casting Jesus in this surrogate role created an opportunity for Octavia to reconstruct her ideas about men. He was perfectly and safely involved in her daily affairs, yet divine and removed from this world. She idealized him and cast him in the role of a safe intimate partner who was also comforter and provider. This healing connection sustained her, but she eventually questioned this surrogate role when she met the man who became her husband and father of their children. One of the things that drew Octavia to him was the way he respected her physical space. Unlike relationships in the past that occurred even before she was attacked, she felt as if he was attracted to more than her body. She was months into their friendship when she felt comfortable enough to share with him that she had been raped and assaulted. His patient response made her feel safe and respected. Their relationship was also significant for her spiritual growth. He was Muslim, and his religious views challenged her notions of God, views of the role that Jesus played in humanity, and the surrogate role that Jesus had come to play in her life. The religious difference, safety, and closeness of their relationship affirmed her search to find God within herself.

Like the women who supported her at a critical time, Octavia was active in the women's ministry and choir. Working through her beliefs about the role that violence played in her life journey was an ongoing part of her faith. She made sense of the violence by focusing on the fact that she had survived, and as a result of having survived, was in a closer relationship with God whom she finds within (rather than beyond) herself.

Camille

"I Don't Know What I Can Do to Get Justice"

Camille is a tall, tawny, brown-skinned woman with bright eyes and a big smile. The conversations for this book were the first time in her adult life that she had ever spoken with anyone outside of her family about being raped by an uncle:

> I remember I was 10 years old. And my uncle from out of the country, he was coming in because he was on military leave. And my mother was so excited that my father had his family member coming over. She was just so happy about it. And he was sharing my brother's room. They prepared the room and everything. So, she was excited. I was excited. And he stayed—I don't know how long—it was a long time. It was a long time he stayed. But, he was always calling me [nickname omitted]. I can't stand that name to this day. "[Nickname omitted]." And one night he asked me to come into his room. So, I came into his room. You know I'm looking at the medals and he's showing me the things he's achieved while he was in the military.
>
> I was looking at it. Okay. That's cool. That's cool. And then he touched me on my butt. And I was like, "okay"? And then...So, I felt uncomfortable and I left the room. I left the room. That night I remember it was dark. And I remember him on top of me. And I just remember it hurt. It was a hurting sensation.

It was hurting. And that was it. I remember coming down for breakfast and he wouldn't look at me. He would not look at me. But, I looked at him. And it was...I remember us going to the doctor. And I remember the doctor—because I didn't tell my mom. I didn't tell anybody and I remember the doctor was saying with my physical exam that I had had sex. And the doctor was asking my mother, "Were you aware?"

Because now that I think about it (because I have a 12-year-old now) that they do annual checks when they get 11, when they're about to go into sixth grade. And my mom said, "No, I didn't know she was having sex." And he was like, yeah, your daughter is having sex. My mom didn't know the doctor was calling DCFS. The doctor called DCFS because she didn't know. And so my mom was asking me what happened. What happened? And I told her that it was Uncle [name omitted]. And I remember her telling my dad what had happened. And I remember a whole bunch of people coming up. His brothers coming up. Other than that it was a blur. I remember going to [name of hospital omitted]. I remember the rape crisis center. I remember that. I remember being separated from my home. I didn't understand what was happening.

I didn't understand. I just really shut down and I repressed it. I kind of just put it in the back of my mind. The only thing that reminds me of that incident is this song, "I Keep Holding On." I just remember that song from that incident. And I knew it was 1985. That's all I can remember from it.

Now since I thought about the incident...My dad had recently got diagnosed with cancer. And I guess while you're on the bed you feel like you're going to die and you start letting out woulda, coulda, shoulda's. And he told my mom, "the incident that happened with Camille when my brothers came up, they gave me $400.00 for you not to press charges," because they wanted him to go back into the military and continue his life.

At times the group conversations were revelatory and affirming for Camille because the other women's stories helped her realize she wasn't alone. At other times, though, she struggled with feeling overwhelmed by the onslaught of painful feelings that came with breaking the silence about incest. Being in the presence of other women created a communal space for her to reflect on what happened to her as she listened to what they too shared. All of the women were at various stages in their self-awareness and healing journeys, but this first time of sharing outside the family was really tough for her.

Camille was a divorced mother of two children. She carried her shapely figure with a sense of confidence that testified to the work she had done over the years to feel comfortable in her body as a woman. It seemed that she had recently come into a space of raising questions and making connections between being raped in childhood and battered in adulthood, and her psychological health. A key moment in her self-awareness happened during the group's first gathering. After all of the women had shared their stories, I invited them to think and speak about a moment in their journeys when they realized they were able to persevere through the pain of trauma that came, left, and often-times resurfaced again. I asked them to share about a moment when they realized they were "going to make it." Camille talked about a song that she'd always made a point to push out of her mind whenever she heard or thought of it, but in this new space of reflection, she heard the song differently:

> The moment when [I knew] I was going to make it through? Remember I told you about the song, "I'll Keep Holding On"? I do believe that was God telling me that "you will keep holding on. Just keep holding on." So, I had to actually get that song and just play it all the way through... [I was] like, "what is this song?" And that's the only thing I could remember from that song.

For Camille, "holding on" meant pushing through the resurging memories of the rape she experienced, and she was clear that it was God who was speaking and encouraging her through the song. "Holding on" also meant being willing to acknowledge that while these horrific events were not all of who she was, they were indeed a real and significant part of her life. As painful as it was, she was willing to hold on to her awareness of what had happened and no longer repress the awful assault. She found support to hold on to this painful piece of her life story through her relationship with a supportive African American female pastor. Their relationship and her attendance at this particular church was a turning point for her:

> I knew the moment I would "make it through" was an encounter with my pastor when I tried to take away that piece and produce myself as a half a sheet of paper. And she told me that, "Camille, you need the whole sheet of paper." And I was like, well, I don't want to tear off a piece. She was like, "no, we need the whole sheet of paper."

At one point Camille had taken the painful parts of her story and torn them out of her life narrative like unwanted pages ripped out of a book. That the encouragement to be "whole" (to own all of her story, for better or worse) came from a female was especially important. Her religious authority proved to be a powerfully positive connection for Camille. The relationship and encounters she had with this female pastor had an empowering tone to them that was absent when she talked about connections with other women—most notably her mother.

During her pre-screening session, Camille mentioned her mother's extreme remorse over her brother-in-law's violence. Her response to her mother vacillated between anger, wanting justice, and just wanting to forget about the entire situation. Camille also struggled deeply with sadness and anger toward her mother over the violence she saw her mother endure at the hands of her father. It was this violence, in fact, that kept her mother from being able to testify in court against Camille's uncle and rapist. Camille had also experienced an abusive marriage and her son was the impetus for her to leave the relationship. One day his words held up a mirror, "Mommy you don't deserve this." She left because she heard her son, knew that he was watching, and didn't want him to grow up and believe that violence was a normal part of love.

Camille's approach to healing and self-recovery centered around her capacity for self-reflection about how the sexual and physical violences she experienced impacted her psychologically, and how it also impacted the intimate decisions she made about men. She would turn inward to reflect, but the inward reflection was often matched by an outward move to seek out encounters and relationships that affirmed her. She found that affirmation in her relationships with women at her church, but she also valued the connections she experienced when she listened to Black female soul artists:

> I listen to music; I listen to music, to express love, healing, power. I listen to songs for attitude. My artists are India Arie, Toni Braxton, Mary J. Blige, *oh God Mary J*. What's the other one? I think those are the three basically...
>
> ...I love music. I love music but the lyrics got to mean something. I just can't listen to any kind of music. So, I had brought one of the lyrics with "Work That" with Mary J. Blige. Anyone have the lyrics to that? Can I read it to you? Can I read it, please? [The group nods and welcomes her] Okay. We all know, *Work That*. It says...
>
> There are so many girls
> I hear you been running from the beautiful queen that you
>   could be becoming
> You can look at my palm and see the storm coming
> Read the book of my life and see I've overcome it.
> Just because the length of your hair isn't long and they often
>   criticize you for your skin tone...
> [I] want [you] to hold your head high cause you're a pretty
>   woman.
> Get your runway stride on and keep going.
> Girl, live your life.
>
> That's just the first one, but it's...You know, I get my attitude from songs, you know? My, "Whatever" [flipping her hand backwards and rolling her eyes]...You know? [My] "What? He gonna say that? He'd better go on." You know, that kind of, [rolling her eyes], you know? I get it through music. (Camille laughs).

These positive lyrics and the images they conjure of a confident, self-loving Black woman helped her not only to gain language and attitude that support the posture she sought with men in her life; they also helped her to heal the shame and low self-esteem that coalesced around her identity in the wake of being raped:

> But, when I listen to the songs and [hear], you know, "pick your head up." You know, "you're pretty, you can do this," you know? Toni Braxton, you know, "He wasn't man enough for me." You know? So I'm like, okay, he *ain't* man enough for me. You know? And then, you know, India Arie, you know, "I'm not the average girl in your video." You know? So, okay, yeah, that's me, you know? So I gravitate toward the songs to build.

The church was a significant place of healing for Camille because the relationships she had with the women there encouraged her to "build" and care for her whole self—mind, body and spirit. When she watched the women in the dance ministry she felt as if their body movements and their praise spoke to issues like the pain that she and other women had endured and the will to be in communion with God, regardless. She pondered joining the praise dance team, but she was undecided because she had a hard time envisioning herself (her body) praise dancing.

During her participation in the research study, the most urgent issue for Camille became what to do with the increased level of self-awareness that came about when she broke her adult silence and spoke about being raped as a child. She attended two of the five research conversations and began informally withdrawing from the research after the second group interview. After several attempts to reach her, we finally talked. When we connected, she spoke about how difficult it was for her to manage the feelings that got stirred up when she broke her silence. We talked things through, and she was open to considering support, and was receptive when I shared the information for counseling options.

Reflecting on Experience

When I looked back at how the women I interviewed met their needs for emotional, physical, social, and spiritual support, I found that only a few of them turned to formal and/or secular psychotherapy and counseling. Instead, they drew on everyday practices that empowered them:

- relationships and conversations with women (elders as well as peers) whose advice, wisdom, and practical support helped them critique and disrupt the imprint of culturally accepted, violent behaviors and patterns
- desire for connections with women that mirrored back affirming images of womanhood, while simultaneously disrupting the flow of heteronormative, racist, and sexist stereotypes
- commitment to noticing God's presence in the everydayness of life as evidence that God had a purpose for their lives, which subsequently affirmed that they indeed bore the imprint of God's own image—even if that image had been covered over by the pain of multiple and various assaults
- development of physical practices (sewing, dancing, singing, using affirmations, writing, meditating) that grounded them in an embodied spirituality that helped them to reclaim their bodies as the site where they encountered God, and through which they (re)interpreted life
- religious exploration of traditions beyond Christianity and integration of insights from these traditions into their identities as African American Christian women
- sharing their stories of struggle and "making it through" with others, which also helped them reframe the role and prominence in their lives of the traumatic intimate and cultural violence they had experienced

These relationships, encounters, practices, and processes empowered the women to actively engage and navigate the cultural, psychological, and theological dynamics involved in self-recovery from intimate violence in a cultural context that demeans Black women. The way they approached self-recovery and healing also directed my attention to areas in which the struggle was ongoing.

When I explored the impact of the interconnection between intimate and cultural assaults, I began to wonder what more the fields of pastoral theology and pastoral care and counseling needed to learn about the inner workings of the strategies listed above before we could presume to be able to care deeply and well for Black women who had experienced intimate and cultural violence. Furthermore, I wondered what I would find when I tuned into the psychological, spiritual, and social/cultural threads weaving in and through their lives and identities. My sense was that I would begin to discern the meaning-making structures that undergird them psychologically, as well as the spiritual beliefs and practices that frame their sense of self, God, and community. These structures, beliefs, and practices are the foundation for hearing Black women's interiority and developing care that matches their worldview. I follow this path of listening, questioning, and analysis in the discussion ahead, beginning with the next chapter's exploration of the psychological and cultural themes that came through in our conversations.

2

Navigating the Hostile Terrain of Intimate and Cultural Violence

The women's narratives indicate that intimate and cultural violence go hand in hand, and that healing requires attention to both areas. For whose initial experience of violence occurred when they were young, the difficulty in this healing is that the violation often had serious implications for their childhood ability to create boundaries and evaluate danger that often persists into their adult relationships. A second difficulty in healing is that given the ubiquitous nature of stereotypes about Black girls and women, the relational and cultural context within which they approach healing is embedded in hostile attitudes toward their race, gender, sexuality, and class. The women I interviewed responded to this challenge with coping strategies and connections that allowed them to survive and maintain their lives. I examine these processes in this chapter, including their perspectives on how sexual violence impacted their intimate decision making, and relationships/encounters that helped them navigate the hostile terrain of negative stereotypes that showed up in places and relationships that were important to them.

Empathic Failure

Collectively, the intimate violence that the women I interviewed had experienced involved childhood incest and molestation and adult rape and battering. Five of the six women were incestuously abused by members of their family or extended family network. While legal definitions of incest may not acknowledge extended family members as perpetrators of incest, I choose to do so in this discussion because of in many African American families, non-blood relatives are valued and trusted just as much (if not more so) than blood relatives. The youngest incidence of abuse began at age three. The remaining member of the group was an adult.

Given the number of women who shared about intrafamily abuse at an early age, I begin this discussion with an exploration of incest from a Self psychological perspective that identifies it as a deeply painful, empathic failure in which the basic human need for mirroring that affirms one's humanity is denied, resulting in grossly distorted images of self, and self in relation with the world. In Kohutian terms, we turn to selfobjects (people) and cultural selfobjects (language, institutions, art, public figures) for empathic connections that positively affirm our existence and uplift our capacity to thrive. We develop such connections through various transferences, at least two types of which are relevant to this discussion:

1. Mirroring selfobject transference: The need to feel recognized, affirmed, and confirmed as a whole person, the need to feel accepted and appreciated.
2. Idealizing selfobject transference: The need to experience oneself as an extension or part of a respected, strong, and admired person.[1]

Empathic response to the need to feel confirmed as a whole person (mirroring needs) and uplifted by a powerful other (idealizing needs) affirms our humanity and place in community. Conversely, empathically failing responses to these basic mirroring and idealizing needs reflect back a distorted, less-than-whole vision of one's humanity. Violence of any kind is an empathically failing response to the inherent need to have one's humanity affirmed and uplifted. Within this framework, when selfobjects commit intimate violence, and/or cultural selfobjects normalize intimate violence, a form of empathic failure occurs and negatively affects the self, meaning one's identity, internal cohesion, continuity, and interdependent notions of self in relation with other. This empathic failure often has developmental implications. One of the areas wherein the implications of the empathic failure that takes place in incest and other forms of childhood sexual assault became clear was how it distorted the women's image of themselves in relationship with those who abused them, and subsequently impacted their capacity for healthy boundaries, and safe/affirming decision making regarding sex and partnering.

In incest, the abuser establishes control over the victim in a way that globalizes his or her presence in the child's life. As a selfobject, the representation of the child's self in relation to the abuser is split off into 'all good' or 'all bad' experience. As the bad images of the abuser and the self are disavowed and repressed off into the subconscious, grandiose images of the self and abuser emerge as a protective defense. In her work with incest survivors, Laura S. Josephs observes, "If a psychologically vulnerable child is hungry for an idealizeable figure, hungry for a powerful person to whom she can be connected in order to feel special and important, then this child may be willing to bend over backward emotionally, to disavow large portions of her own experience to obtain and sustain this experience of idealization."[2]

Joseph's observation helps us make sense of the conflictual patterns of behavior that are often misconstrued as the child's, or adult survivor of childhood incest's efforts to protect those who abuse them. The effort isn't directed at protecting the abuser, but rather to protect oneself against intensely painful distortions of the self caused by incest. The psychic material contained in the repressed split-off portions of sexual abuse is so unbearable and psychologically threatening that awareness of the abuser as the source of the pain they experience is repressed in favor of maintaining the idealized images of self in relation to the abuser. For Cirene, this dynamic surfaced in the jealous feelings that began to develop when she saw the girlfriend of the cousin who had been abusing her. The traumatic nature of the attachment with her cousin became the basis for how a fantasy of their relationship unconsciously emerged to overshadow the pain, shame, and terror she experienced in his violations:

> My cousin [who] would often isolate me from family members in order to molest me was in high school when the abuse occurred. I came from such a trusting extended family that to be left at home with just a couple of people including my cousin was not seen as a big deal. The first time I experienced oral sex was with my cousin in the downstairs bathroom at my grandaunt's house. I even remembered feeling a very deep sense of jealousy and anger when my cousin brought his girlfriend home and wanted to be locked in a room with her and not myself. I remembered being a pest, always trying to come between their relationships all in attempts to secure my sexual place with him. The emotions are what I remember the most and so is the long-term depression.

Eliza also shared about having idealized her abuser. Like Cirene, she was significantly older before she could verbalize the contradictions in the incestuous relationship with her father:

> I thought for many years that my father was the most amazing man in the world since he could do anything that needed to be done. He could sew and knit and even crochet. He was an excellent cook and even did some catering. He always had a job and for the longest time I wanted to have my man, when I was old enough to have a man, to be like my father. While I was a chaplain intern at [name of hospital omitted] it came fresh/anew to me that I had been a sexually abused child. I connected with this when I had to write a myth for reflection. In my piece I reflected on the fact that my beloved father had treated me like I was his wife, his woman, his bitch, or his whore...
> And then I remember when my first little titties showed up, "Ohh. I have to tell my daddy." Now isn't that funny? No remembrance of the sexual abuse. No, but daddy was my star and I was his. And I wanted to tell him and I said that in front of my stepfather and he thought I meant him. And I said, "Oh no, I don't want to tell you nothin'." So that's when they put me out of there. So you know, my stepmother put me out first and then my stepfather put me out the second time. I was always a difficult personality.

With Cirene and Eliza, the abusive relationships were important selfobjects around which they built a "strong sense of
specialness"[3] that overshadowed conscious awareness of the
abuse. The overwhelming nature of the abuse that Cirene and
Eliza experienced required repression of the bad images of self
and abuser to fend off the unbearable conscious awareness of
sexual violence. This complex defensive intrapsychic function is
especially important in incest, where the offending selfobject is
a relative—someone trusted by the child and other members of
the family. The abuse in incest takes on a global and totalizing
effect because in the child's eye, the silence that it engenders
implicates the entire family.

The offense is deepened when the child speaks up to someone else in the family who then denies or is complicit in the
abuse. The effect is that the abuser takes on such a large presence that the child faces little choice but to idealize the abuser
and the images of the self in relation with the abuser, rather
than consciously acknowledge the possibility that the entire
family is aware, but does nothing to stop the abuse. The long
term effects of the intrapsychic maneuvers that allowed them
to survive incest in childhood can be observed in their coping
strategies, attitudes they developed about sex, and in the stories
they shared about adult rape and battering by males they knew
and oftentimes loved.

Rori, Tamara, Eliza, and Camille all discussed attitudes
they've held about sex, which shed light on the impact of childhood intrapsychic defensive mechanisms (like dissociation
and repression) that continued even into their adult intimate
encounters:

(Rori) After experiencing the sex by force so many times I
eventually decided that during the initial rape act I would give
in...tell my heart and body that, "He is not going to take it
from me anymore. Just give it to him and force him to fuck you
right." That really never happened that way. I began to associate
or replace the idea or feeling of love with having sex. I thought
that would give me back my power. But it did not. As a matter
of fact I was not sure of what power I was taking back.

(Tamara) I have always divorced myself from my body because I tend to be very careless with it in terms of sexual interactions and so it was always "a man can have my body," but that doesn't mean anything, because he doesn't have my mind, and so as long as you don't have my mind then I'm not really totally invested in this thing.

Camille's story was slightly different in that rather than dissociatively severing the connection between mind and body, following her rape, she unconsciously invested all of her energies into sex as the act that would bring her love.

(Camille) Yeah, because it was a time where I didn't feel pretty and—especially after the incident because I just didn't. And when I was in a relationship with boys I would cry my heart out and my Mom would say, "Camille, why are you crying so much?" You know, and I thought that sex was love. So when it broke up, you know, I was all in pieces because I gave what I had, you know? I gave what I had. So at first I didn't understand why she would, you know, "Why are you crying?" But now I think, "Why am I crying?"

For all three of the women, intimacy—rather than the sexual act itself—became the primary threat to their emotional stability. They did not want to experience physical and psychic pain, so they engaged in sexual encounters from the dissociative position of having already separated their hearts and minds from their bodies. While the survivalist nature of how they engaged in intimate encounters provided the most vulnerable part of their psyches (the part that needed nurture, care, and protection) with a modicum of security, it did little to support them in developing relationships where their safety (mental, physical, or sexual) was not an issue. The implication is that traumatic selfobject experience, in particular transmuting internalization of one's abuser as an empathically failing selfobject, has developmental consequences that oftentimes manifests in repeated connections that involve various forms of abuse.

Of the five women who were abused as children, four shared stories of repeated rape and battering in their adult relationships.

The easy explanation for the patterns of violence in their lives is to simply pin it on shame, low self-esteem, or a passive acceptance of abuse. However, these simple responses overlook the formative influence of traumatizing selfobject experience in which representations of oneself in relation to an important other are idealized at the expense of one's own self and conscious awareness of the selfobject as a violator.

Judith Herman describes the adult patterns of violence for childhood victims of sexual assault as the phenomenon of repeated victimization in which intimate relationships may be simultaneously driven by hunger for protection and care; fear of abandonment or exploitation; dissociative defensive styles that make it difficult to form conscious and accurate assessments of danger; and the wish to relive the dangerous situation and make it come out right.[4] Through a Self psychological lens, each of these behaviors is interpreted as "transference repetitions of those childhood experiences that interfered with the normal development of the self."[5] But, the aim is neither to recreate the violence nor to intentionally place themselves in harm's way.

Rather, the unconscious motivation is to seek out relational contexts in which they hope to have an empathic selfobject experience that differs greatly from the original traumatic representations of the self in relation to other they experienced in abuse. The goal is empathic connection rather than further abuse, and when patterns of abuse in later life emerge (including abuse of other loved ones like their own children in which they are either complicit or directly responsible) the genesis of these patterns should be traced back to empathically failing selfobject experiences (including empathically failing parents and other caregivers who failed to intervene) rather than innately flawed intrapsychic structures as has been the disposition in some classic psychodynamic views.

The women I interviewed discussed how two categories of women (OtherMothers and Sisterfriends; Cultural Craftswomen) helped them learn how to disrupt cycles of intimate violence by interrupting the secrecy and normalcy that surrounded incest and other forms of intimate violence. These OtherMothers, Sisterfriends, and Cultural Craftswomen were also instrumental in disrupting the flow of cultural attitudes and messages that normalized the violence in their lives. I begin with the first group, OtherMothers and Sisterfriends, to cultivate an understanding of the role that everyday intimacies between Black women play as critical sources of healing and power.

OtherMothers and Sisterfriends

OtherMothers are the women (grandmothers, godmothers, aunts, and other women in the community) who are not birth mothers and are oftentimes unrelated by blood, but who shared the responsibility of nurturing and providing guidance in the lives of the women I interviewed. In *Black Feminist Thought: Knowledge, Consciousness and the Politics of Empowerment*, Patricia Hill Collins describes these female bonds and the role they play in providing collective communal support for Black girls and women.[6] On the subject of OtherMothers, she recalls, ·

> In many African-American communities, fluid and changing boundaries often distinguish biological mothers from other women who care for children. Biological mothers, or blood mothers [sic], are expected to care for their children. But African and African-American communities have also recognized that vesting one person with full responsibility for mothering a child may not be wise or possible. As a result, OtherMothers [sic], women who assist blood mothers [sic] by sharing mothering responsibilities traditionally have been central to the institution of Black motherhood.[7]

For Black girls, the care that Hill Collins describes includes developing self-definitions that empower them to resist negative cultural views of Black femaleness. Black feminist psychologists Tracy Robinson and Janie Victoria Ward describe this resistance as a necessary aspect of Black female psychological and cultural development:

> African American adolescent girls, [like] their Euro-American counterparts, are engaged in the process of identity formation

and self creation....However, African American adolescent girls [who] are making this passage embedded within a family and community...[are] negatively impacted by a sociopolitical environment in which she will live by fostering development of a resistance that will provide her with the necessary tools to think critically about herself and the world and her place in it.[8]

OtherMothers are important conduits for lessons on how to resist and claim spaces that are different from the ill-fitting spaces created for Black female selves in culture. Taken together, Hill Collins, Robinson, and Ward's perspectives highlight the role that maternal figures play in challenging distorted cultural projections of Black female identity. Their comments primarily focus on the impact of individuals and institutions outside of the African American community. What their comments do not engage with is OtherMothers' roles in challenging deleterious experiences that occur *within* the African American community. My analysis revealed OtherMothers as influential resources in this social critique. For these women, healing from intimate violence also involved recovery from hostile cultural attitudes that impacted their sense of self in society and especially in their own community. This became apparent in the analysis of the narratives of those who experienced sexual violence at an early age.

For three of the five women I interviewed, in childhood as well as in their adult lives, OtherMothers were key mirroring selfobjects whose responses to abuse and other matters related to their sexuality and intimate choices differed greatly from that of their birth mothers. This was especially significant for the women whose mothers didn't believe them when they reported abuse; held religious and social attitudes about gender that implicate women in their victimization; whose own personal trauma was a barrier to the daughter's safety; or whose concepts of female gender were strictly heterosexual. In each of these circumstances OtherMothers provided important mirroring selfobjects through which the women experienced nurture that affirmingly reflected their worth by acknowledging the pain of abuse and rejection.

For Rori, the responses to abuse and violence that she received from OtherMothers were vastly different from her mother's denial. When Rori told her mother that an extended family member was molesting her, her mother did not believe her. Instead her mother protected him, "No, don't be lying on Uncle [name omitted]. Don't lie on him." While Rori's birth mother didn't believe her, her aunt did. Acting in the role of OtherMother, her aunt confronted Rori's birth mother. Her aunt's own experience as someone who had already survived incest compelled her to tell Rori's father who in turn confronted the abusive adopted uncle. Rori's truth-telling brought about empathic resonance in her aunt (a mirroring selfobject) who reflected back the sadness, rage, fear, and betrayal that Rori felt. Her response addressed the co-occurring intimate and cultural violence that Rori experienced, first, in being raped by a family friend, and, second, in being discredited as a victim in a culture that routinely absolves perpetrators of violence, especially when the abuser is male and a clergy person. Her aunt's empathic resonance affirmed Rori's humanity at a painful time in her life, and the memory of those moments with her OtherMother significantly affected the internal images Rori held of herself as a woman.

The response from Rori's mother to the abuse prompted Rori to question whether or not she could trust and confide in her mother about violence and pain she experienced from those who were close to her. That ambivalence developed into reluctance by the time she was an adult, and it was again an OtherMother who helped Rori sort through what had happened. This time she had been battered by a man she was dating. When she didn't feel as if she could talk to her birth mother, her godmother and several OtherMothers in the church were willing to hear her. They stepped in to help her escape from the relationship:

> I drove to my mom's home, for that is where I had left my son so that I could go out. After I reached my mom's home I was glad that everyone was sleeping. When they got up for church I yelled downstairs to let them know I was upstairs. I did not want my mom to see what had happened to me. I knew she would cry and want to give me the church message about

staying with someone you are not married to. She would try to justify that that was punishment from God. She would then say, "at least God did not allow him to kill you child." But my godmother from the same church had a different response. She said, "Baby, don't allow no man to whoop you. No woman deserves to be whooped by a man." She began to tell me ways to get back at him. Ways to get away from him and the foolishness. He never hit me again but I was busy getting out of his apartment, his space and his life. Women from the church who had been abused began to circle me with their love, compassion, and understanding.

Rori did not talk about the assault with her birth mother because she anticipated that her mother would use religion to justify the abuse, claiming it was God's way of punishing her for having sex outside of marriage. She realized, however, that she was not left alone to deal with the trauma of being beaten by someone she loved. These OtherMothers to her adult self responded like her aunt did to Rori's childhood self. They mirrored Rori's distress back to her, and by their practical actions affirmed that she was worthy of protection and support. A key reason behind the authoritative status that these OtherMothers held in Rori's life was that they belonged to the same church as her birth mother, but held different beliefs about womanhood and God's stance on violence. These women filled Rori's need for intimate connection with a mother figure who was able to respond with empathy to her emotional angst over the violence done to her.

Like Rori, Eliza also struggled to receive responses from her birth mother that would affirm and empower her in the face of abuse. Eliza described her mother as an abandoning figure who chose men over her welfare, leaving Eliza feeling unprotected and unwanted. "Fortunately for me, they kicked me out of the house and I was raised by my grandmother, the widow of Reverend [name omitted]." In the one-on-one interview she explained further, "That was my salvation because I would have been a prostitute. I probably would have been on the street in drugs and alcohol. 'Cause what else did I know?"

Her grandmother was the pastor of a local storefront church that became a second home for Eliza:

> So, I spent my Sundays, Wednesdays and Fridays at [name of church omitted]. Service was held in the parlor of the former home for unwed mothers. There was rooms rented upstairs to old folks who lived in [name of city omitted]. My first crushes were with the boys at church. My first sexual encounters, with the older men in the neighborhood. You know, the bad boys who hung on the corner at the little community pool hall. My neighborhood was in the suburbs of [name of city omitted] but church was in downtown, rough and poor. But, these were the people [who] were served and these were the people who loved us and with whom I was in constant companion. I taught Sunday school. I was the Sunday school secretary. I sang in the choir. I played the piano with one hand to give us a tune. I first shouted just like my spiritual mother who could hit high C and turn like a top.

For Eliza, the church became a place of refuge from her father's sexual and emotional abuse and her mother's abandonment, while at the same time providing her with important relationships in which she felt acknowledged and esteemed. The move to her grandmother's home didn't completely protect Eliza from violence. In the previous chapter we heard her recollection of being coerced into a sexual act by a stranger on the street. However, it did provide a significant degree of refuge.

At first glance it is clear how her grandmother met Eliza's mirroring needs, but she was also an important idealizing selfobject who uplifted her in terms of how she came to a healthier understanding of her place as a woman in society. Eliza warmly recollected, "Grandma, (name omitted), kept the church going. Service was who she was and who I became because of what she had shown me about serving God." Following her grandfather's illness, her grandmother took the reins and led the church's efforts to meet needs in the community. As a Black woman leading a church in a working-class neighborhood during the fifties, her grandmother's work and disposition represented an idealizing selfobject context. Eliza saw her not only as her grandmother, but also as a public figure in the community, whose use of resources and leadership placed her outside traditional gender roles. When the discussion in group interviews turned toward ideas they encountered about women's roles in society in general, and church in particular, Eliza's comments differed greatly from those of other group members. While many of the women mentioned dominant cultural messages about women's subordination, Eliza spoke about the strength, courage, and beauty of women's leadership. Those comments were a clear reflection of her grandmother's (OtherMother's) influence on her as an idealizing selfobject who encouraged Eliza's drive to pursue her goals.

Sexuality is a third area of support where OtherMothers were alternative maternal selfobjects. Navigating sexual development is a challenge for all adolescent children. However, the task is far more complex for children whose sexual maturation takes place against the backdrop of sexual trauma. This was the case for each of the five women interviewed who were assaulted as children. However, Cirene's story raises awareness of how social biases in families related to female sexuality can add an additional layer to the complexity. Cirene's birth mother and grandmother initially rejected her lesbian identity, and the rejection was a serious blow to Cirene's understanding of who she was and the conditions under which her family and the wider community would embrace her:

> I think my anger for this really came from my family, from my mother and my auntie. "If your grandmother was alive—she'll be turning over in her grave," and "You know, what kind of example are you setting for your little cousins?" And it always went back to that perception of the family. And I remember I used to tell my mother stuff out of spite…"Oh, yeah, me and my girlfriend had this argument," or "Me and my girlfriend did this," knowing she didn't wanna hear about it. Half the stuff probably wasn't even true, but I just wanted her to keep hearing me say "girlfriend, girlfriend, girlfriend," over and over again, because I knew that it hurt her….I wanted her to feel the same way that I felt, and so, but after a while it probably started to smooth over, and even me and my sister, we were very playful. We were very close

growing up—we're still close. And after I told my mom that I liked women. I don't know, I was wrestling with my sister and I was on top of her or something, and she was like, "Get off your sister! Get off your sister!" She's never told me that before. And I was like, "Oh, you're thinking my gayness is gonna come off on her?" Like, I just couldn't believe that she just said that stuff. And "Oh, you wanna protect your precious little daughter. I'm not trying to do anything to her that's out of order." And, so it was just stuff like that, the little things like that that made me feel uncomfortable, that made me angry, that made me even wanna pursue it more, if that makes sense, because of the way that she felt about it, and talked about it. But after a while, in 2008 maybe, she was just like…she came to the conclusion, "You know what, if this is the lifestyle you're gonna live, just don't bring it in my house or around me, and don't talk about it around me." So we're still at that point right now…we're still at that point right now.

Her birth mother's refusal to accept her sexuality denied Cirene an important mirroring selfobject experience that would affirm her as a whole human being. The unempathic response to her emerging lesbian sexual identity added a layer of complexity to her sexual development that also included making sense of being raped. Her response was to seek support from other female mentors (OtherMothers) in her church community. There she was able to "come out" under the guise of needing help with homosexuality and talk openly about the abuse in her past. The support she received was mixed. In one instance, an important mentor and OtherMother acknowledged her orientation but asked her not to come out to members of the mentor's new women's ministry. Though these experiences provided more mirroring than her encounters with her birth mother, they also mirrored back distortions of her sexuality. The OtherMothers would not connect with the parts of her that did not align with their heterosexual norms. This was especially significant and disturbing since these women were the nurturing presences who provided a safe space for Cirene and were able to hear about the abuse, anxiety and depression, cutting (self-mutilation), and drug and alcohol abuse.

Rori, Eliza, and Cirene's narratives point to how maternal relationships that are often not linked by blood between Black women are important and oftentimes complex selfobject contexts in which these women experience mirroring that nurtures and empowers them in ways that their birth mothers would not or could not. The implication is that OtherMothers (grandmothers, Godmothers, aunts, fictive kin, and mentors) are especially critical when birth mothers do not believe reports of abuse, hold religious and social attitudes that block them as confidants, or whose own personal and cultural trauma may be barriers to providing safe and affirming environments for their daughters. In this case, OtherMothers provided selfobject milieus where the women could merge with nurturers who cultivated emotional and practical tools that empowered them to interrogate distorted self images they had developed because of the abuse. These mirroring and idealizing experiences (especially in the case of Eliza's grandmother) did much to empower the women to critique messages they received within the African American community. Cirene's narrative, however, also directs attention to sexuality as a key area in which even as they attempt to provide support, Black women continue to struggle to accept one another holistically.

Unlike the other women who sought out OtherMothers, Octavia found support in women who offered connections that were nurturing, but not maternal. Her birth mother and grandmother were very supportive. But, while she needed safety and comfort like anyone else would in the face of violence (regardless of their age), she didn't look for the same kind of maternal guidance that the other women did who were young at the time of their initial assault. She found Sisterfriends, women who offered a non-maternal, yet deeply intimate and supportive presence. I use the term "Sisterfriends" to describe the non-blood ties that exist between Black women who share the load of providing care and practical support in good times and bad. Importantly, they are often peers in age who provide intimacy that women may or may not experience with female blood relatives. For Octavia, her Sisterfriends provided a level of care and comfort that helped her handle the shame and onset of posttraumatic stress related to her attack.

When Octavia was gang raped, she did not want anyone to know about it. Yet, despite her best efforts, she couldn't hide it. Though local media reported the assault, Octavia managed to maintain a degree of anonymity until a close friend realized she was the woman in the news reports. When the friend called to let her know that she knew, Octavia was both relieved and horrified. She didn't have to carry the secret alone anymore, but this one friend was part of an even larger circle of girlfriends who would soon find out too. Even though Octavia was horrified, she found comfort in how these girlfriends gathered themselves around her to make daily survival doable:

> And what really helped me was having sister girlfriends to always love me. One of my friends always walked me to my car when I'd get off the train from work. We rode together. And she would always walk me to the car because I was scared to even go to my car a lot of times. And she did that for, I'd say, a good two or three months. I just got a lot of love and support. And that helped to build up my self-esteem.... They didn't say, like, "What happened?" Or, "Why were you with him?" Like I say, no judgment. They were just like, "What do you need? I'm coming over. Let's do this. Let's go shopping." Because they know I couldn't go anywhere alone. They were just there. They were just there. Sometimes they would call and just pray. Just call and, "I just want to pray with you," over the phone.

This mirroring was crucial because it confirmed that the attack really had happened, and it acknowledged her horror. Walking her back and forth to her car and their intentionally non-judgmental stance were critical aspects of the Sisterfriends' care. In her personal statement Octavia wrote, "My sister-friends were so reassuring and convinced me that I did nothing to incite this incident and that it would not prevent me from having future viable relationships with men, as I believe[d] i[n] the beginning." Rather than silence her or blame her for the assault, their responses helped her rebuild the self-esteem that sexual assault took from her, while also providing a safe context for her to re-examine, and gradually reconnect with her community.

In Octavia's experience of Sisterfriends, as well as Rori, Eliza, and Cirene's experiences of OtherMothers, we see Black women's analysis of their place in society, and their everyday efforts to meet survival needs as key elements in psychological healing. While they could not protect the women from every threat, their empathic responses helped the women through their suffering in ways that had a positive intrapsychic impact.

Cultural Craftswomen

Women's healing from intimate violence also involves recovering themselves from cultural practices that normalize violence committed against them. Far from existing as benign ideas circulating in culture, systemic notions of race, gender, class, sexuality, and power contribute psychological material to the relational milieu within which these Black women's ongoing psychological development played out. Paying attention to how Black women locate internal and external resources for navigating this hostile terrain is important because it sheds light on the interlocking nature of cultural abuses of power that can only compound the sense of powerlessness that comes with intimate violence.

The images, achievements, and public presence of popular and professional women were important resources in the women's recovery from the cultural violence that co-occurred alongside their traumatic experiences of childhood molestation, rape, incest, and battering. In much the same way that OtherMothers and Sisterfriends provided selfobjects contexts that mitigated the impact of intimate violence, "Cultural Craftswomen" (cultural selfobject) provided another important resource for resisting cultural violence. By Cultural Craftswomen, I am referring to female figures and artists who engage public space through artistry and acts of service as a matter of craft. Their craft consists of their creative and professional efforts to secure public and communal space in which the work they do disrupts the effects of oppression against women.

My notion of the Cultural Craftswoman builds on Kohut's idea of cultural selfobjects as idealizeable figures who replicate for groups of selves in culture what occurs in the individual developmental context.[9] Through acts of service and civic office as well as performance on public platforms, they offer practical wisdom, visual imagery, and spiritual insight that uplifts women in ways that empower them to survive, heal, and take up agency in resisting a culture that normalizes violence against them. Though less intimate than their relations to OtherMothers and Sisterfriends, these nonetheless highly influential encounters with Cultural Craftswomen challenged cultural practices that perpetrate emotional violence against women. They were instructors, leaders in church, choir members, social service providers, actresses, singers, writers, and preachers whose images and works inspired the women at various points in their self-recovery.

Tamara's narrative demonstrates how cultural selfobjects prompted her to cast a critical gaze on systemic prejudices that influenced the racial perceptions she held of herself. For her, Black female opera singers embodied ideals that disrupted the dominant cultural narrative about appropriate spaces for Black bodies and voices in performing arts, and in the world in general. In spite of racism these vocalists and performers strive to carve out a space for themselves and their voices in a genre that is largely dominated by Europeans and European Americans. By excavating this under-told history, Tamara grounded her musical talent in a legacy and developed a sense of racial pride that buffered the cultural alienation she often felt:

> I started looking for music by Black composers and then I started finding out that, you know, we've been doing this all along. You sit. You listen to people, "You know black folks don't do opera, what [are] you talking about? Why are you singing that stuff?" And it was like, "Yeah, but we do." ... And then there was this woman, I forget her name, her last name is Story, but she wrote a book, And So I Sing,[10] and it was a history of black female opera

singers. And she started back with a woman, Sissieretta Jones, and somebody Greenleaf and she's talking about how Greenleaf comes out and performs and she was a dark skinned woman and they didn't even talk about her singing, they were talking about her Negroid features and how ugly she was because she had a wide nose and it was just...But this was like maybe right after slavery or still during slavery. And so—but that was what they were talking about and they were telling...They were talking about her as a trained, you know, just like a trained animal. And I remember I was—but it reinforced this idea that I hadn't just popped out of some nebulous place, you know?

Sissieretta Jones was an important, historic, Cultural Craftswoman onto whom Tamara projected her need for an idealizing selfobject who faced, challenged, and transcended racism. Jones and others Tamara researched were subjected to racism, but they persisted in their art and were able to claim public space for their Black bodies and voices in spite of it. The legacy of Black female opera singers who achieved success provided images and narratives that uplifted Tamara's sense of pride when she faced criticism from within and beyond the African American community. She was often accused both of being too Black to sing opera, and of not being "Black enough" because she sang opera, all of which occurred alongside the prejudice she encountered about the color of her skin. Tamara had lighter skin, and the intragroup prejudice that she experienced in the Black community was part of an underlying speculation about how her skin color or hair texture were indicative of how she related to other Black people. These artists, however, were sources of uplift that supported Tamara in claiming an empowering space for her body and voice as a Black female performer in spite of this intragroup struggle.

The women also recognized Cultural Craftswomen in female figures who were not always Black, but in whom the women found images that uplifted them in terms of how they perceived their value, and the cultural roles assigned to them as women. While Cirene mentioned one Black girl group (TLC) and author Maya Angelou as influential cultural selfobjects, the remaining

six female figures (singer, Alanis Morissette; "Designing
Women" television sitcom character, Julia Sugarbaker; Xena
and Gabrielle from the television series, "Xena: Warrior
Princess"; and Michaela Quinn, the principal character on
the television drama series, "Dr. Quinn, Medicine Woman")
who were significant figures for her are white women. Here we
observe in action Kohut's claim that we know the meaning of
cultural selfobjects by the functions they provide for the groups
they represent.

What drew Cirene to these women was not so much the need
for racial uplift, as it was her need to feel uplifted about her
gender and sexuality. In Morissette, Cirene experienced mirroring that she needed—the free expression of rage over abuse
that she wasn't allowed to voice because of shame, fear, and her
father's demand, albeit unaware of his daughter's rape, that she
"stop all that crying." Her father dismissed her taste in music as
basic teen rebellion, when in fact far more importantly she was
drawn to this particular female performer's sound because her
music spoke to the silence that women are forced to endure in a
culture that does not take them seriously when they try to speak
their pain. In a culture that normalizes violence against women,
females are often discredited as overly emotional regardless of
what incidents may have caused them to become emotional
in the first place. The music gave Cirene permission, a voice,
and an outlet for the rage she felt over her cousin's incestuous
assaults on her.

In addition to rage, Cirene was very much in touch with her
feelings of powerlessness and quite possibly abandonment by
her family. She dealt with these feelings by idealizing images of
those who voiced their rage, and of those who took actions to
reclaim their power from painful pasts. Xena Warrior Princess
was one of these characters:

> If I could just be like her because I thought she was so power-
> ful, so courageous. She had this confidence that she just went
> around just like righting wrongs and it was all about redemption
> within herself, the whole story was. And how she had this life
> that she wasn't so proud of and then she found _____ salvation

and she was just trying to right her wrong life or whatever. And I just thought that she was so fearless and so courageous and she was really, really so powerful, she didn't take anything from anybody and so like, I would go out, and I'd take a broom stick, like I had a sword _____, you know, fight against trees and stuff like that or try to fight with my sister. My sister [would say], "You're not Xena."

Xena's need to redeem herself from a painful past by standing up for others struck a chord in Cirene as she struggled with the shame of sexual abuse. Cirene watched this character for cues on how to redeem herself and reclaim her power. In Cirene's narrative, these Cultural Craftswomen were idealizing cultural selfobjects with whom she merged to take in as sources of strength that enabled her to reject invisibility and silence:

So Julia Sugarbaker, like, she was my favorite character, like and I really...I just loved her sassiness, I loved her class and she was another woman that really represented power to me also. And she had this confidence that was out of this world and she didn't take anything. And for the longest, I just thought like through my molestation, like I gave away my power. And so looking back over it, I watched shows or emulated characters who just took total control of self. Had like this total control of power, this total control of confidence. And Julia Sugarbaker, she just really represented that for me and she was very articulate, very classy and she just came at it with the *mouth*. And so for the longest, even as a child, I just had this crazy mouth. Always talking, kind of talking back. Like at school I was real passive, but at home I was very kind of aggressive. Passive aggressive, more so...Always kind of talking back...Yak...yak...yak... yak. But I come from a family of women talkers anyway. And I just thought she was very cool...So—and I just thought she was very cool and then my next character was Michaela Quinn off of "Dr. Quinn, Medicine Woman" [group laughter]. Right, I was really into TV. Yeah, right, like I was really into fantasy, like fantasy just really helped me to feel. It was like an escape. So I was coming up with characters in my head and I was like, "Oh my God, what if she was my mom or what if it was back then, what character would I play?" And so her, she was very smart, very articulate and she was very confident.... And she always did what she thought was right, no matter what the consequences were. And so like, I really, really admired kind of like the strength that she had, even in a character. And so those are like, the three main characters that I really looked up to that kind of really helped me through, you know, adolescence and young adulthood and teenagerhood just watching those shows. And really kind of taking, pulling strengths from them and pulling different techniques from them, like, okay, what if I just did this, maybe it would just work out like on the TV show.

Each of the characters she described either physically or emotionally embodied characteristics that defied culturally produced depictions of women as weak, docile, dependent, submissive, or feeble. Cirene described her connection to these characters and female images as part of a fantasy world in which she merged with them to experience ideas about power and embodiment that uplifted her sense of womanhood, this despite the gender norms in her family and religious community that enforced rigid gender constructs that also implicitly condemned homosexuality. Gender norms like the ones at play in Cirene's narrative demonstrate how families either mediate or mitigate cultural norms. Cultural Craftswomen provide important alternative narratives that empower women to transcend these cultural norms, that often exists in their close relationships.

Female social service providers and professionals working as Cultural Craftswomen in the public/civic spheres were also significant to these women in terms of influencing them at critical decision-making moments concerning their health, safety, and well-being. Consider Rori's interaction with her female therapist and an attorney:

I remember when I went to the thing before I left [name of city omitted]. As a matter of fact, the therapist was one of the people who gave me the final thing that told me you need to find a new place because your children are afraid to come outside. When you speak to them they are afraid to... When you speak of his name, they are afraid that he's around and that he's been watching and that he's been coming down the street, driving by... Just trying to inflict fear in them when they were coming up... So, the therapist during that time had to explain that it would be better if I could [get] out of town. [She asked] "Did I have any other place to go?" And that's when I started checking around with family members to see who lived where and how far away was it...

During this time Rori was working in the offices of a woman lawyer to bring in money. This woman also represented her during legal hearings related to the violence and harassment Rori and her sons experienced with her former husband. This attorney had been very supportive not only as an ally, but also as someone who was in a position to offer employment to a working mother who was trying to build up resources and change the course of her life and that of her children. This support and practical advice were vastly different from what she experienced when she turned to the criminal justice system for help with the abuse. Her husband's position in the community as a fireman and civil servant provided cover for his violence. Although she had pursued the proper legal channels, members of the judicial community colluded with his violence, leaving Rori feeling disregarded and powerless. With the money she'd saved from working in her attorney's office, and taking her counselor's advice, she gathered her resources (internal and external) and fled her abusive husband:

When I moved here, I had to move in the middle of the night because there was a court order that was supposed to stop me from leaving town with my son that had been molested by his father. And because I had worked for my lawyer that week for part of my pay, for part of her pay because her secretary was out, I was able to see the paperwork that was coming in. And I saw that Thursday that there was an injunction filed, but she was not in her office and she wouldn't be back till Monday, so she wouldn't have gotten it anyway. So I told them, we're leaving Friday night because... I say [to myself], I have to complete this week, but we are leaving Friday night.

And I had an '80 Pontiac and I packed a little cooler. And clothes for them, like a week's set of clothes for them. My sewing machine. Because I said, and some fabric. I say, "I know wherever I go, I can make me some clothes to do whatever, but you all are going to need something because you know your clothes may not be accepted. I want you to be accepted wherever you go in the northern schools." And I had a cousin who lived here and asked him could I come up. I shouldn't be able to…I shouldn't have to stay with you no more than six months I said, because I have a degree, I should be able to go into any place and start working. And I had a little money because I had my two checks, whatever I had written all my letters and sent them out so the lady I was working for could hopefully find another worker. And um, asking her, telling her thank you for the experience or whatever and not to uh, not to worry about us. We were going to make it. We just needed to leave immediately. And uh, when we did, that Monday the lawyer called me and said, "Rori, did you know about this injunction?" And I said, "Huh? Pardon me?" And she was a saved lady and me being saved she knew I wasn't going to lie. I said, "Uh, you talking about that one at the bottom of your paper that you wouldn't have got to till Wednesday?" She said, "Yeah." I said, "Yeah, so I figured if you didn't get it to give it to me, then it didn't count." She said, "Well, you knew that much of the law." She said, "But you know, um, he's going to try to fight it." I said, "I know he can, but we're already here now." And uh, so running in the middle of the night like that, looking out for what I had to look out to protect my children because he was a fireman. And with him being a fireman, every time his name came up in the court system, they dropped it. He, you know, he could do whatever he wanted to do and it was okay. And he had promised me he was going to kill us or he was going to take the kids. Dispose of their bones so much, dispose of their bodies and dissolve their bones and stuff so nobody would ever even find them. I had never even heard of this kind of foolishness. So I was like, no, you can't do that. And my baby was afraid. He had slept with me for three years after we moved here. And that was part of his therapy. I didn't get much sleep because [he] had kept having these nightmares. "He's coming mama. Mamma, he's here!" And then he would call in the middle of the night. So, I had to change my number and I [inaudible]…threats. [He said] "I'm coming." I said, you come on because [name of state omitted] is looking for a Black man like you. He wants you to come here.

So, he never came. But, he was just constantly trying to torment us. And I was like you ain't getting the best of me, I'm so sorry. I [inaudible] keep from killing you and I'm not going to let you come here and steal me from my children.

Recall Sheppard's awareness that "cultural selfobjects are not solely individuals. They are also the symbols, language, institutions and cultural productions that meet those needs for individuals that are sometimes embodied by individuals."[11] As a cultural selfobject, the legal institutions Rori encountered symbolically represented groups that routinely absolve males who use violence against their family members of being held accountable for their offenses. The multiple institutional obstacles that victims of violence face in their attempts to receive support and justice in cases of intra-family violence like battering and incest include civil servants and judicial authorities who hold victim-blaming views of intimate violence; police officers' refusal to take intimidation and/or damage to property seriously as criteria for making an arrest on an intimate violence charge; and requiring that children bear the weight of establishing their own credibility in cases of adult abuse committed against them. Rori faced these cultural assaults, and although the legal system failed her, both the therapist and her attorney provided her with important responses that differed greatly from cultural norms and systemic practices that normalize violence against women.

While at first glance they simply appear to be mirroring selfobjects, a closer looks reveals them as Cultural Craftswomen. Yes, the therapist addressed Rori's and her children's immediate safety needs. But more than physical safety was at stake in these moments. The equally important concern was Rori's encounter with this woman's ethical commitment to disrupting violence as an ideal that uplifted Rori in the face of cultural norms that sanction women's disempowerment, subjugation, and forced dependency. Recall that Kohut identified cultural selfobjects as "creative persons in religion, philosophy, art and the sciences who are in empathic contact with the illness of the group self and through their work...mobilize unfulfilled narcissistic needs and point the way toward vital change."[12]

For Rori, this therapist functioning in the role of cultural selfobject was in touch with violence against women as a group
illness within the culture. Her therapist's advice that she take
her children and leave represented an empowering cultural selfobject experience with a mental health institution that conveyed
hope that there were parts of society and community that do
indeed prioritize women's safety and rights. Similarly, the attorney also provided an important idealizing cultural selfobject.
This woman's legal practice functioned as an institution that
provided Rori with the legal insight and financial support that
ultimately positioned her to take her children and leave. When
the attorney made room for Rori to work and earn money as
a temporary secretary, she uplifted Rori by creating an opportunity for her to gain resources that further empowered her
to be an agent in, and work toward, the safety of her family.
The attorney was a cultural selfobject who understood wom-
en's unacknowledged intrapsychic need for collective resistance
against systemic processes that sanction and collude in violence
against women.

Female cultural selfobjects like this and the others described
above surfaced as images and representations that offered lifesaving insight and life-changing alternative perspectives at critical
moments. These selfobjects and cultural selfobjects were highly
influential mirroring and idealizing resources that impacted how
the women interpreted and responded to the sources of violence
that shaped their views of themselves, and helped to shift the
women's interpretations of the violence committed against them.
Healing and self-recovery necessarily involved drawing on the
kinds of psychological, social, and communal resources that were
present in the positive selfobject and cultural selfobject experiences detailed above. It is in these resources, as well as others,
that these women and many like them found pragmatic support
and psychological resources. Amassing these kinds of resources
and supports was critical and life-saving, yet these resources
alone were not enough to help them thrive holistically.

Holistic healing and recovery also involved their faith. Faith
was the platform and context for them to work through the

meaning of God's presence, absence, activity, and inactivity in intimate and cultural violence. I consider this faith in terms of how it helped them critique the church as a mediator of cultural violence, see their distinctly female selves in the image of God, and make meaning of violence in the following chapter.

3

A God I Recognize

One of the most nefarious aspects of intimate violence is its capacity to negatively impact how Black women view themselves as bearing the image of God. This first challenge is followed by a second blow that occurs when important religious communities mediate (rather than mitigate) the misogyny that sanctions intimate and cultural violence. Conversation with the women revealed that healing from this double-pronged attack could only occur when they began to notice and question the double-binding nature of the church as a place that nurtured them on the one hand, while simultaneously socializing them into gendered and sexual norms that they later found less than helpful in healing from intimate violence. This chapter examines how the women wrestled with a sense of alienation from God, self, and others in light of this dynamic. The narratives suggest that interrogating their theological heritage to reconstruct their spirituality, and embodied spiritual practices allowed them to retain a salvific vision of a God they recognized.

Interrogation

When the women explored the contours of their spiritual journeys, a review of the religious messages they received as children and adults helped them see how religion mediated cultural violence through misogynistic/patriarchal gender norms, and what impact those messages had on their relationships with, God, self, and others. The women identified the church as a formative and foundational source of their spiritual consciousness, but it wasn't until they interrogated the gender and sexual socialization they received from the church and members of their religious communities that they felt genuinely connected to God. This interrogation allowed them to examine the validity of gendered social norms and religious messages in light of their lived realities as Black women who experienced violence and yet believed in God.

Their introspective gaze often fell on messages they received about the shape of the social space carved out for them. This was an especially important point of exploration for the four women who sensed God's calling on their lives to actively pursue some form of ministerial leadership. Cirene reflected back on the particular impact these messages had on her while she was discerning God's calling on her life to be a minister:

> And...but that church thing, even that call to ministry, like I always felt restricted, restricted, restricted. I always felt myself wanting to rebel, because I couldn't understand....Okay, I have an arm. Yes. How is that so sexual to me, you know? And when people pull me aside "Oh, you're...." I mean, if I have something like this [pointing to her short sleeved top] on [in] the pulpit...[They say] "Oh, your arm is out!" Really?! I mean is it really that distracting to you? I just really, really can't stand that. And it's always on the female's response...Not on the male's response of, "you know, well, control yourself or learn how to have a little grace and class." It's always, "Well you should do this, you should do that." Because men, men, men, men, men and I never hear them getting the talk.

For her the church was an intensely anti-body space that overemphasized controlling female bodies and sexualities. This antagonism is both exaggerated and exacerbated for women whose gender and sexuality furthers the antithetical nature of their presence in leadership spaces traditionally reserved for married, heterosexual men. Cirene was neither male, celibate, nor married, and her developing lesbian identity significantly challenged all three dimensions of these gender norms in

Christian tradition. She encountered these views from both men and women who openly chastised her, as well as through less-obvious social codes that dictated norms for how she should present her body both inside and outside of religious space. The messages suggested that something about her body was unholy, requiring that she cover up and carry herself in a manner that concealed her embodiment (inclusive of her sexuality) as if it defiled sacred space. While several of the other women experienced similar sexualized sanctions on their bodies, the experience was amplified for Cirene because of the additional stigma against her same-gender loving identity. Although it put her at odds with members of her family and church communities, she refused to accept the asymmetry in how female and male bodies and sexualities were regarded in church. Cirene's interrogation clarified the traditional Black church as a mediator of cultural messages that regulates Black female embodiment. Her reflection created a context for her to re-examine the criticism she encountered as evidence of the community's (not God's) discomfort over her embodiment and sexuality in sacred space.

Whereas Cirene's reflection focused on the church's role in regulating women's bodies, Rori's examination unearthed explicit claims in the church about God's part in controlling female sexuality. She became clear about the gender norms that justify different sexual codes for women and men as the underlying concern in the God language she often encountered. For Rori, sexualized sanctions against women's bodies showed up in her sanctified church's teaching on the Holy Spirit as the binding force that prepared women for marriage by helping them remain virgins or maintain abstinence:

> We used to always ask, "Okay, so the Holy Ghost the men get is different than the one the women get?" Because the one the women got supposed to have us under control and the men, we still got to cover up and stuff for them? I mean...I'm like, what is it with all this?

Rori believed what she'd been taught: that if she was a good woman (which was determined by her lack of sexual activity) God would send a husband who would honor her in marriage.

Waiting to have sex equaled holiness; and holiness meant that their union would be blessed. She waited until she was married to have sex with her first husband, but she began to question the teaching about the Holy Spirit when he became violent:

> But, then I look at the other relationships, like with my second husband or my first husband...My first husband....And, how you love somebody and then you find out they're molesting your children and *you* at the same time. That's craziness. And then getting it then in the church at that time...You're thinking, "Okay, Lord, I've done this right this time. I've waited and got married and the whole nine yards." And then this foolishness happens. So then you're saying, okay, so that ain't the answer. So, it's a lot. I mean, you think you've gone past it. You look at it. Look back over it. You whitewash it again and hang it back up and you still see spots. Just constantly working on it. It's a constant thing to try to be made whole from this. It's a constant work. Yup.

Looking back Rori realized that her decision to abide by the church's gender expectations concerning chastity and holiness did not prevent her husband from abusing her. Because of the pain and the dissonance, she rejected what she'd been taught and instead developed a belief in the Holy Spirit as a presence that sustained her in the middle of painful circumstances. She no longer thought of the Holy Spirit as being overly focused on her sexuality. Instead, Rori developed an understanding of the Holy Spirit as a protective presence that sustained her to the point of being able to muster enough internal (spiritual and emotional) and external resources (a concrete plan, including money) to leave her abusive circumstances.

For these women, encountering the disruptive nature of Black women preachers and pastors in the pulpit proved to be a significant factor in their processes of interrogation. Yes, they attended church to worship God, but the interviews revealed that they came away with more than just a worship experience. They came away with a certain sense of uplift in their spirits that was specifically related to encountering a woman in a pastoral position of authority. Clearly, these female pastors were important idealizing cultural selfobjects to the women I interviewed, but they also played the role of demonstrating God's regard for female humanity and the Divine's will to show Herself from within distinctly female bodies:

> *Cirene*: As I got older, I think that the art that really saved me, that really helped me progress was really the art of watching women preach [agreement from others in the group]. And watching my mentor. She received a call in 2003 and I remember joining her church in 2003, and when she got behind that pulpit and even the way she walk [*sic*] and carry herself. I mean, her cadence, her confidence, and we were....By ourselves, she was saying, "Oh, I just felt that I didn't do a good job." *I* felt like that was a confidence. I was like, "What? But you just seemed so poised, you just seemed like you took control, you seem so powerful," and she was like, "Yeah, but I figure I should have said A and B instead of D and C," or something like that. And just really, really watching her progress in ministry and really seeing the power and really seeing other women just really being drawn to her for her gift and art of preaching. Like, I really, really looked up to that and I really admire that thing that was within her. And I think that really helped me throughout my young adult years to find a sense of peace and like, "Wow," you know? Because that was when I was experiencing my call, too and I just remember just looking at her even behind the pulpit and just seeing her like just really, really glow and coming into herself. And so I just really found power in that.

> *Camille*: I just wanted to comment on Cirene when she said...[Turning to Cirene] When you saw your female pastor, I think that was the opening eye for me, for my journey in healing. Because once I saw my female pastor I was like—I was looking at her like, "I mean, she's doing this, she is doing this." And just to see her, you know, just do her thing and talk about God and, you know, and how she was flowing. I was like...I said, "I hope I'm not getting prejudiced here." Because a male preacher preach...I would just totally—it totally—I wasn't receptive, I wasn't hearing. But moving to another church and I was like, "Well, he ain't got _____, I'll _____ ask her, she got _____ _____ _____, she got all _____ _____." But that was definitely a journey for me. After seeing her I was looking at her like a child at Christmas. You know, like, you know? I don't even know what that is.

Cirene and Camille spoke specifically about the women's bodies (the way they moved, how they stood, the sound of their voices, the words they chose), which subsequently affected what they believed about God's positive regard for their own bodies. As women claiming pastoral authority in spaces historically dominated by men, the positive and transformative activity of their voices and bodies in public space demonstrated God's presence in Black female bodies that are often sexualized by the church and subsequently dehumanized by a culture that condones violence against them. These images were important *imagos* that reflected back possibilities for the divinity within their own humanity if they would only dare to recognize God's enlivening presence in their distinctly female bodies. Memories of their encounters with women in the pulpit provided them with tangible evidence of God's will for women, which subsequently lifted up the possibility of their own female bodies as mediators of God's presence. Echoes of these memories and their impact on how the women rejected gender-biased cultural norms could also be heard in Eliza's memories of her grandmother's powerful pastoral leadership in a small, urban, storefront church. It also showed up in Octavia's recollection of a church soloist, whose voice let her know for sure that God existed and expressed God's own self through female bodies.

A Reconstructed Spirituality

The impact of these memories and *imagos* is best observed in how they propelled the women's active decision to reconstruct their sense of spirituality around the particularities of their experience with God. For Cirene this active use of agency took her down the road of pursuing formal theological education, and a search for God that took her beyond the Christian traditions. Cirene's hunger for spiritual knowledge began in childhood, but her intellectual nature took on new meaning during college when courses in religious studies became more than intellectual exercise. Education was a critical dimension of her spiritual journey. In addition to presenting her with information that challenged gender norms veiled in religious language, the courses also provided opportunities to challenge what the church taught her about God and suffering. Two particular experiences during this season of her life significantly influenced how she viewed herself and what she believed about God. The first was her introduction to Buddhism and the theological contrasts she noticed when she compared its language and practices to those of what she experienced in the Christian tradition:

When I was at college, my first time taking a Bible 101 class, and I got a C. And so, I was very disappointed, because I thought. "I've been to church all my life, I should pass this class with an A." Well, that's when I realized that God and the Bible wasn't all that my family and church had taught me, and that's when I really started to fall in love with, I think, the whole culture of the Bible and spirituality and religion. That's when I started taking tons of religious study courses, because they really, really opened my eyes to see this whole history in connection with the people who got in the Bible. It started to have a history and a beginning point, and God didn't just fall out of the sky. And so, I started to take a "Women in the Bible" course. And that's my first time meditating in a Buddhist temple. I really fell in love with that type of spiritual system. Even throughout junior high school, like, you know how you have religious studies that force you to kind of see different religions. Buddhism was something that's always just kind of stuck out to me, and I fell in love with it, because it was a thing.... They always talk about peace and tranquility and Nirvana, and Christianity was always *picking up your cross*. It was always a lot of suffering, a lot of suffering language, and then not a lot of peace language to me, and I just didn't like that. So, meditating in a temple, which is like...You know, "just sit, relax, and whatever you feel, whatever you want to say, feel free to say it, there's no judgment here." They were very welcoming....Like "no, judgment...." [There was] no, "you don't have on a skirt...you have on pants"....I mean, it was just like, "Come on in." I was the only black person there, but it was just like a welcoming experience. And so, God really started to open up.

The language and sense of community she experienced in Buddhism was more comforting and welcoming than what she experienced in the Christian communities she had lived in. This was especially significant given her struggle to make sense of the role that suffering from incest played in her spiritual development and relationship with God. Buddhism provided her a lens to through which to interrogate messages in Christianity that emphasized the primacy of suffering in spiritual growth and development. Her Buddhist exploration led her to a place of self-acceptance that emphasized God's non-judgmental presence, which was critically different from the shame and judgment that characterized her previous beliefs about how God viewed her.

Her second experience significantly challenged what she had been taught as a girl about the gender of God and what this subsequently meant for her to be created female in God's image. She recalled the college boyfriend who used the Bible to prove his point that God was female. It was the first time she ever considered that God could be female. Although she didn't believe him at first, she took the information back to the women in the family who nurtured her faith:

> I mean, that stayed with me. I remember exactly where we were standing in his house when he first told me that. He had the Bible open. He was like, "No, God is a woman. Like you should see this. Like I don't understand why you don't see that." I really thought that he was crazy. And then, I remember going back to my mentor, my auntie, and I was like, "Have you ever heard that God is a woman?" [She said] "Oh, yeah, child. God is a woman, da-da this, and da-da-da." I said, "Why you never told me this?" Like, I don't understand why did I have to experience that type of knowledge outside of family and outside of church? And so, it was a common thing. I'm thinking like this is stuff that this guy is really making up. I really felt bad being in his presence, like I should[n't] be here. And they [the women in the family] were like, "Oh, yeah. We heard of that, and God can be a woman if you look at A, B, C, and D." I was like, "Well, I don't understand why this lack of knowledge thing is going on here in the family."

This discovery made Cirene aware that while the women deferred to male privilege in the church, this deference was actually a matter of subversion. Their affirmation of God's femininity blessed Cirene's continued religious interrogation, which took her to seminary where she explored Ifa and Voudou (African derivatives of Yoruba culture, both of which feature female and male deities).[1] These perspectives informed the African-centered Christianity she settled into as the foundation for her work in ministry. Each of these experiences offered Cirene exposure and knowledge that empowered her to interrogate her own early formative teachings in the Black church by broadening what she knew and believed about God in general, and in particular what it meant to be created female (and good) in the image of a God who is as much female as male.

Cirene was not alone in exploring religious traditions beyond Christianity as part of her process of reconstructing a spirituality that spoke authentically to her genuine connection with God. Octavia explored Catholicism, Islam, and Buddhism after she was gang raped. It was a weeding-through process by which she too developed an appreciation for the femaleness of God, a notion that challenged what she had been taught in her Baptist church upbringing:

> I started praying differently. Praying differently and asking this God, whoever God is, and at that time it was like a "man." It was kind of like a man, not necessarily a white man, 'cause I didn't see like a face when I prayed to God. It was just kind of like a space where I went inside myself, you know, trying to get to this man. Always trying to get to this man. And I think that kind of confused me (trying to get to this man). I would look at earthly men and say, "Well, maybe that's a way to kind of get to God." Having a good relationship with a man, not necessarily any particular man. Just, you know, believing in God is probably good enough. Just kind of a weird...
>
> Well, that's really what led to the event that happened with my friend—[name omitted] is his real name...So [name omitted] didn't really go to church but he seemed like a very nice guy. Handsome. He was, you know, pretty successful. A gentleman. He just kind of looked like that model of what this God that I was trying to have a relationship with would be. So, I said I can't really figure out how to have a relationship with God ('cause I

prayed but it doesn't seem like anything really happens when I pray). So I said, "[God] help me to find a man." Here comes [name omitted]. I'm like, "Okay. All righty." And I just kind of put a lot of my energy into him (thinking that would help me understand God better). And when that didn't happen, of course, I was devastated…And the incident happened. Just a whole lot of things. So it was then, Stephanie, that I learned that there's only God. There's only God. Because it's like the Spirit said, "You misunderstood. You misunderstood who I am." Who *we* are. Because I'm like hearing all these things. Like, "it's not about a man." That was like the first thing: "See, you really was trying to get to this man and you see what happened to you?" So it's kind of like the feminine energy was trying to teach me something. Like, look, get back inside. Come on back inside yourself. Don't look for a man. Just come on back inside yourself and try to build up a relationship with yourself again and that will help you get to me. So, then I didn't really know who me was. Who was trying to talk to me? But, I knew it wasn't a man. I knew it wasn't a man.

Octavia was in therapy with a female counselor during this time of exploring religious traditions and re-examining her relationship with God. Counseling (outside of the church) provided a space where she could step back and look at how the male imagery and language she experienced in the Black church context affected what she believed about herself in relationship with God. On the one hand some of this language was very helpful. The maleness of Jesus was very important for her as she dealt with dating fears concerning rejection and further violence:

After I was assaulted I didn't think a man would want me. That was like a really big thing because I felt for some reason they would just know (like I had "rape" brandished across my forehead or something like that). So, I had, you know, [a] really hard time with that. But knowing that there was Jesus…I'm like, "Okay, Jesus is gonna accept me. Jesus won't do that. Jesus is gonna be my man. Jesus is gonna be my man and I'll be okay with that." Because I don't have to worry about when I meet an earthly man, is he gonna figure it out? Is he gonna notice something? I just don't even have to deal with it. So if I stay away

from them, I can still have a man [((Jesus)]...Because that was
still important, you know, to have that relationship, you know,
but I don't have to deal with those kind of issues because Jesus
is not there. You know? Not physically there. So there's no, like,
rejection. There's no...I don't have to worry about is he gonna
come on to me, is he not? You know? Things like that.

For a while, Jesus was her surrogate "man" who met her
needs for safe companionship and acceptance. He was the Jesus
who "knew all about it," and because he had his own experience of unjust suffering, he could come and be with her as companion, savior, and protector. In this regard, the Black church's
emphasis on the maleness of Jesus as a fundamental aspect of
his humanity proved to be critical. She needed to be "saved"
from the horrific memories of gang rape and the threat of more
pain. On the other hand, she still wrestled with how male God-
talk thwarted her efforts to envision a connection with God
inside of her distinctly female self.

She had turned inward in search of God, but the male imagery and language handed to her about God was a barrier to her
sense of herself as a vessel for God's presence because she wasn't
male. Exploring Islam, in which the historical male Jesus is not
regarded as the savior through whom all believers are redeemed
and connect to God, was a significant part of this turning point.
She managed to draw on Islam's de-centering of Jesus without
re-enforcing the patriarchy that runs through both Islam and
Christianity as Abrahamic faiths. This was an important aspect
of how she drew on what she learned from other traditions to
interrogate and challenge male-centered language from her conservative Baptist upbringing. When she adopted theological language that mirrored back the fullness of her distinctly female
humanity (inclusive of her body) as a reflection of God's femininity, she was able to let go of the belief that rape was a divine
punishment for missing the mark in her relationship with God.

The interviews revealed a dialogical process in which the
women trafficked back and forth between their childhood and
adult experiences of God-talk, culture, and religious community.
Becoming able to hold the oftentimes opposing views embedded

in these memories helped the women seek out a God they recognized. Their interrogation allowed them to envision themselves at the center (rather than on the margins) of a relationship with God. It allowed them to see clearly the misogynistic and patriarchal elements of the Christian tradition they had been handed, to which they responded by charting new directions less obstructed by God-talk that oppresses and obscures God's active presence in women's lives.

Enfleshing Power

Reconstucting their Spirituality involved more than a cerebral sorting through of multiple messages and encounters. The women also had to *do* something to mediate this spiritual connection with God. Prayer was a central part of this reconstructed spirituality, but it was often accompanied by practices that embodied the women's decision to pursue and maintain a connection with God. This spirituality occurred in and through their bodies, and it was a source of power that strengthened them holistically (in mind, body and spirit).

Octavia talked about *affirmations*[2] as a form of prayer in which she deliberately spoke positive energy into her consciousness and environment, to proclaim her belief in God, commitment to community, and hope for her life. Her first exposure to the power of making affirmations occurred through Ifa priestess Iyanla Vanzant, whose writings continue to be popular with Black women seeking support and advice on self-recovery from various wounds (personal, cultural, and otherwise). She was reading Vanzant's *One Day My Soul Just Opened Up: 40 Days and Nights Towards Spiritual Strength and Personal Growth*[3] when she had a spiritual breakthrough that changed the weight of the grief and trauma she had been carrying from being viciously assaulted. The affirmation encouraged Octavia to consider how she could exercise agency in manifesting God's presence in her life and what that presence could mean for how she valued her own presence in the world. The one she shared in the group interview focused on her identity as a child of

God, and her body as a vessel through which God made God's self known to affect the conditions of others positively:

> I found this book and would read, you know, the affirmation just to really, you know, help myself. And I was sharing it with my sister today. I would like to read it just... "Today I recognize that I am a child of the Divine, sustained by divine love, guided by divine light, protected by divine mercy, alive through divine grace."
>
> And that was the part that, you know, I really had to focus on, "alive through divine grace." I love Iyanla, you know, because I feel like she is definitely, you know, one of my sisters in the spirit because she's been *through*....If you've ever read her books, I mean, she's been through it all.
>
> "Today I am thankful for this gift of life through which I'm able to serve. Today I ask the Divine to use me, use my mind, use my eyes, use my ears, use my hands, use my feet, use my being and this gift of life to serve those in need."[4]
>
> And when I pray I usually ask for that covering for eyes and even for breath and hands and I forgot about my thumb, I guess. But, you know...Because I just realize that, you know, if you're alive today, you are so blessed. I mean, you just don't know. When you come *this* close to death and you staring at death and you can't do anything about it. And then you survive through it and you don't think you're worthy, you know?

Octavia's narrative suggests that her use of affirmations is somewhat different from traditional prayers in which the emphasis is on God's initiative and activity. While claiming God as the source of her strength, the affirmations engaged the power of her will and her physical voice (even her very breath) to join with God in co-creating change. The affirmations also linked her personal growth and power to positively impacting others as a way of honoring (perhaps even worshipping) God's presence in her life. This affirmation was particularly influential in her healing and self-recovery because through it she reclaimed her abused body as a sacred vessel in and through which God lived and acted.

Dance was another embodied spiritual practice that mediated a connection with God. This was especially important for Tamara who continued to use dance in her pedagogy as a middle-school teacher. She began taking dance classes as a child, but dance took on spiritual significance during her college years when she took African dance classes with devotees of Santeria and Voudou:

When I got to college, I started taking African dance, and I did that for years. The woman who taught me—the two women that taught me, one of them was really into—she went really off into Voudou.

And so, I remember [name of instructor #1 omitted]—it was [instructor #1] and [name of instructor #2 omitted]. [Instructor #2] was my first teacher, and she was like 300 pounds, but she was really all into Voudou, and Santeria and all of that. And so, the things that we got from her, the dances and things, were from that perspective. When [Instructor #1], who was her teacher, began to teach me, [Instructor #1] was 71. That woman could dance you under the table. She would look like, "What? Where you at? Come on. We got stuff to do," and I'm like gasping for air. But, she was all about the spirituality of it, but she didn't practice it. So, we would do the dances, but she would always purposely believe something. She was like, "You don't want to be calling nothing up in here that you ain't got no business calling." Whereas [Instructor #2] was just like, "Okay. Well, let's just do it," and she didn't really care. You didn't know what you might get. So, [Instructor #1], but [instructor #2] was—so, I got really into this whole thing, and it was from [Instructor #1].

I couldn't say this then...Then...I can look back, and it was at that point that I—that it was clear...That my call was going to be my call, was going to be my call, was going to be my call. And it was going to come up no matter what I did. It was just going to be that. So, because I—it just was what it was. [Turning to address Cirene] It was just like you were saying about your uncle. You could see it anyway, and so it didn't matter that what I was getting into wasn't what I had grown up with. What I was called to do was still coming out, and I couldn't say that then, but I could say that now.

Tamara's dancing was an important spiritual discipline in which her body was the medium for experiencing God and through which she fully experienced her whole self. The two women who taught her the sacred dances of Voudou and Santeria were instrumental in helping her to recognize the spirituality of her movements, and by extension, the spirituality of her entire self. Another important aspect of Tamara's dance experience was the non-Christian, African-centered context in which she experienced the spirituality of her body. Both Voudou and Santeria are diasporic derivatives of African traditional religions that feature female and male deities. The theological language embedded in the narratives her instructors shared from these African religious traditions came alive and were a powerful dimension of the dances she learned.

While Tamara self-identified as a Christian, she also acknowledged the role that African dance and exploration of African religious traditions played in awakening spiritual gifts she'd received from God. African dance was one of several embodied practices from which she drew skills and resources to strengthen and ground her faith. Another involved singing spirituals that she had learned from her grandmother who had raised her in the Baptist tradition. These spirituals served the purpose of connecting her not only to God, but also to her grandmother who was a key influence in her beliefs about God's ability to meet her needs. Tamara was not alone in her use of dance and singing as a spiritual discipline. Rori, Eliza, and Octavia all considered their activity in the choir, and even their ecstatic (Holy Ghost) dancing during church service important acts of worship and spiritual practice.

In each of these spiritual practices their bodies were the medium through which they connected with God in their innermost selves. These connections lifted up the sacred nature of their bodies, without the cumbersome weight of misogynistic and patriarchal religious language burdening their efforts to connect with a God they could recognize inside themselves.

An important dimension of these spiritual practices also involved their capacity to simultaneously disrupt cultural violence. Rori's use of sewing as a spiritual discipline exemplified this dynamic wherein the spiritual and the cultural intersected. Rori's mother taught her how to sew in grade school. It was a practical skill that many girls from her generation were expected to learn. However, for Rori, sewing became an embodied spiritual practice that taught her to listen for God's revelation in the seemingly mundane activities of life:

> I started sewing when I was a little girl about um...Yea, they made us sew in middle school, at that time it was junior high. I started sewing then and I would pick it up and put it down until in my thirties. And I saw this African fabric. This fabric, it just call me to go back to sewing. And that's when I started doing it, sewing my clothes again. 'Cause I had this little lanky body then, but the stuff in the store really didn't fit and I was like, "I am not going to be a black Barbie." Oh, [I] changed my hair, changed everything. Everybody thought I had lost my mind (That man done made her go crazy). Yeah....I think that sometimes it was a place not to think or to feel, and another time it was a place to feel and to think when it got real creative, because I remember giving it [sic] strange names to the outfits. When they say, "Where did you get that from?" I said, I don't know, that's what the new fabric say just *call* it. They'd say, "I *know* that fabric ain't talking to you girl." And I said well, kind of like, it kind of tells you what it want to be like, you know, because you try *everything* else and until you get it just the right way....Then it will say something like, "that's what I want to look like." And you be like, "Why you did something like this?" And I said, cuz it didn't finish talking to me. You know, just leave it there. But I think everything speaks to us, it's just how we listen.

Rori started "listening" to fabric about how her body should show up during a transitional time in her life when she was able to reckon with (which is different from surviving) the abuses she had experienced in her life. She stopped pressing and processing her hair with chemicals to alter its texture, grew natural locs, and developed a distinctly Africentric aesthetic that she expressed in the clothing she made. Rori recalled the fabric telling her how to drape itself across her body. An important aspect of this practice was her use of African cloth. She rejected outright European fashions ("I'm not going to be a Black Barbie") and instead created an image for herself that affirmed her racial identity and cultural heritage. It was a spiritual practice that led her to a strategy for interrupting unwanted cultural access to her body and identity. She specifically used African cloth and styles to counter the cultural privilege afforded classic Eurocentric body types, and cuts of clothing that many African American women find ill-fitting.

Sewing was a way to create a physical, mental, and spiritual barrier to the cultural assaults that occur through social scripts about how women's bodies should show up in public space. This was also significant for Rori as an adult survivor of childhood abuse, abuse in which she vividly recalled feeling like she had been dressed up like a baby doll when her abuser violated her and her sisters. Psychologically, sewing allowed her to reclaim her body by giving her the ability to determine how much visual access others would have to her body as a woman. It allowed her a choice about her body—something she didn't have when she was being abused All of this occurred under the umbrella of sewing as a spiritual discipline in which she reinforced her spiritual connection to God.

Dealing with Defilement

Interrogating formative religious contexts and reconstructing spirituality to find an authentic relationship with God were huge elements in these women's healing. But, their spiritual journeys also included the difficulty of dealing with the effects of having been physically, sexually, culturally, and spiritually abused. The remaining portion of this chapter examines the women's feelings of shame and issues regarding justice and forgiveness as ongoing challenges in their relationship with God and their overall healing.

The shame that the women described indicated a sense of not being "right" in the eyes of others (including God). It was a diminished sense of worth that often forced them to retreat from themselves, God, and others. Tamara compartmentalized her feelings and beliefs about how negatively God viewed her. She separated these feelings from other parts of her life because of the globalizing sense of shame she felt around repeated intimate and sexual encounters. During the individual interviews she talked about how the emotional abuse she experienced in her relationships with men resulted in her feeling that at times she embarrassed God.

> *Tamara*: Um, I think we can very definitely say that had I not believed in God, I would have been done. Um, but there is also this constant awareness of not being right. You know, how you want to fix yourself before you come to God and so even though I know Jesus died for my sins. I know that God sees me through Jesus and he's not looking at my faults, per se, but I look at them. And it's just like this, sometimes it's horrifying. You know, it's not the....I don't even know how to describe it, so sometimes it can be very weighty because I have a very difficult time with grace.
>
> *Stephanie*: It sounds like you are also struggling with shame.
>
> *Tamara*: Yes. Um, I was, you know, I don't know if I said it in the meeting, but I know I was telling someone else the other day that failure has never bothered me, so success bothers me.
>
> *Stephanie*: The fear?
>
> *Tamara*: The fear of success. The fear....
>
> *Stephanie*: Being found out later on?
>
> *Tamara*: Yeah, you know how they dig into your past and they you know, bring it out and you know, I'm like I've been there and done that already. I don't really feel like I want to do that again. You know, but at the same time, it's like it's hard because it's in me and I want to be successful and I have this drive to be really good at what I do and successful. But at the same time, I'll sabotage myself so that I'll get almost to the top, but not enough to really draw a whole lot of attention, almost, but not quite and so that's frustrating for me. And so, but you know, I'm trying to, for a long time, I never saw spirituality and my art in the same place, that was two different things. Nothing had, everything was very disjointed in my life and it still, for the most part, is very separate. I have a difficult time integrating all the different pieces with spirituality being over the umbrella kind of to everything coming under that and being a part of it. It's kind of different and out

there and I don't know if it's... I don't know. I just feel like
often I feel like I embarrass God.

Stephanie: That makes me sad. Not pity or shame, but it makes
me sad, you know. It makes me sad with you. It's a sad
feeling.

Tamara: It is and I, and the thing about it is I don't know if I
really believe it all the time. It's like I know enough to know
that that's not it. That, that is something that's really skewed
and off. I know there is something off with that, but often I
am so caught up in it....

Stephanie: You feel it...

Tamara: And you know? Or, I let it direct my actions, where I
find myself, like a lot of times if I fall off the wagon or if I'm
you know, like a... If I have sex with someone and I'm in that
mood. And, then, when I feel like, "Oh God." Again? Really?
Am I there again? And I don't want to come to...you can
confess that I've done this again. And we've already talked
about this and I should be over this and I shouldn't have done
that, so I allow that to [sic] kind of beating myself up to pull
me further and further away, you know, less time reading the
word.

The shame that Tamara struggled with manifested in her feeling that the actions and choices she'd made emanated from her
own internal source of badness. The defiling experiences of abuse
in childhood and subsequent repeated intimate violations like
emotional abuse in adulthood obscured her sense of being created in the image of God. While she claimed that God saw her
through Jesus' redemption, when sex was involved, she struggled
deeply with shame as the lens through which she saw herself. She
also believed it was how others, including God, saw her. Although
Tamara struggled with shame, her relationship with God sustained her belief in a divine purpose for her life that superseded
her shame. Knowing that God had a purpose for her life, in spite
of how violence caused her to question that truth, allowed her to
push back against a shame that nearly overwhelmed her at times.
Like several of the other women, she too held onto belief in God's
divine purpose for her life as an ultimate counter narrative to
shame. This core belief strengthened the women time and time

again to push through the barrier that shame erected in the connections they sought with themselves, others, and God.

Another area in which the struggle to overcome the defilement of intimate and cultural violence appeared was the ongoing challenge they felt concerning wanting justice on the one hand and the expectation (internal as well as external) that forgiving those who hurt them should be a priority in their healing. The women most often encountered this challenge when breaking the silence about violence they had experienced. Each of the women broke the silence over intimate and cultural violence differently. Some opened up in therapeutic settings about what had happened to them as children, and this supported them as they considered confronting family and community members who were complicit in the abuse. Others used less obvious means like the arts (singing, sewing, dancing, and music) as a medium for concealed truth-telling, while still others proclaimed the truth of the abuse they'd experienced openly and directly through public speaking and published writing. In each of these acts, they presented their pain to the community in search of some kind of response that resonated with their outrage and sadness.

It was not unusual for these truth-telling moments to put them at odds with people they hoped would save them when they were children, or provide comfort as they attempted to work through the trauma as adults. Central figures who raised particular tensions for them in this truth-telling process included mothers who didn't believe them, family members who didn't hold incestuous abusers accountable for their offenses, and community members who acknowledged the offense but then used religious beliefs to encourage and justify premature forgiveness without any efforts to hold the offenders accountable. These experiences raised tensions in the women's efforts to heal and recover from the trauma because it required that they essentially deny very real spiritual wounds in order to accommodate the needs of others. They responded to this tension by relying on the truths they unearthed about God. Their reconstructed, authentic relationship with God empowered them to resist religious, communal, and cultural pressure to forgive, forget, and prematurely move along. This resolve to resist manifested in various ways, including clarity that they were worthy of justice—even if they had yet to receive it decades after the original offense.

Camille's relationship with God verified for her that she was justified in her belief that her uncle was wrong and that the family members who protected him should share the blame and consequences of her pain. Maintaining the belief that she deserved justice was a vital part of her ongoing resistance against cultural codes and family behaviors that encouraged her to remain silent or simply move on:

> I suppressed it. When it would come up I would blow it off or whatever. Whatever. And when I see him now—because he is my father's brother—I still see him now. And I'm angry. I'm angry that he did this to me. But I think I'm more upset with my family. I think because I didn't feel like I was protected. I don't know the outcome that came from the incident. I do remember court. When I think about it...I'm starting now to ask my mom questions. And when other family members tell me that he's raped our uncle. When he raped a boy? He's done it again to other people. He's not right. He's not right. And ya'll are protecting him. I don't know what I can do to get justice. I don't know. I don't know if justice was done. My mom tells me that he served two months in jail. But, she also told me that my dad beat her up so bad that she couldn't come to court the next day to testify. So, that's my story.

Camille was frustrated with her family's willingness to risk vulnerable family members in order to protect others who were abusive, and she was frustrated with a justice system that she feels also failed her. Her mother was incredibly remorseful over what happened; however, her mother's apology didn't cancel out Camille's desire to see her uncle go to jail for raping her or her need to hear the family confess to how they had protected him over the years. Camille persisted in her desire for justice. Her faith was a source of strength in this resistance because her beliefs about God's presence in her life allowed her to see her sacred worth as something worth fighting for.

This kind of resolve also presented a spiritual dilemma for some of the other women. While they were deeply convinced that justice should be the family and community's response to the violence, they felt trapped by their own commitment to spiritual views wherein whether or not they would be spiritually released to move forward from the memories and the effects of trauma was inextricably connected to their capacity/desire to forgive those who hurt them.

This dynamic showed up in Octavia's story. Unlike Camille's abuser, legal justice was served when Octavia's offenders were sentenced long term for sodomizing and beating her. But, her comments about what she felt even some twenty years later spoke to the spiritual dimension of the justice-seeking processes. In addition to justice, Octavia was concerned with her offenders' remorse and transformation. She wanted to know if there had been any sense of repentance:

> After a series of court appearances and trial and the whole nine yards, two of the men were sentenced and put in jail. And actually one of them is still in jail, because every so often when he comes up for parole, the parole board will contact me and say, "Do you have any input?" I always write a letter. I always want to know if they have any remorse or what has been their conduct while they're in there. But they're not willing to share that. They're like, "Well, you'll have to go through hoops to find that out." So I just kind of state my case and say it's been 20 years, just about. If there has been some redeeming qualities to this person, I don't want to be the one to say, "keep them in jail."

Octavia wanted to know if her offender had developed an understanding not only that what he had done was wrong, but why it was wrong. In addition to justice, she wanted to know if he had repented—had he turned to pursue a more sacred way of being human and respecting the presence of God in others. An important aspect of this desire concerned possible consequences in her own spiritual journey if her response to the pardon and the parole board negatively impacted him. Her narrative presents a tension between her need for justice and religious pressure to forgive (regardless of whether or not the man who raped her had repented). Octavia and Camille's experiences clarify the tensions that seeking justice create in the spiritual lives of those who experience violence.

Another struggle around forgiveness showed up in the tension some of the women faced from family members when, in adulthood, they refused to be in a physical space or family gathering with former abusers. Tamara reflected back on a time when her mother asked her to stay home with her during a visit from the male cousin who had molested her:

And he had just gotten out of jail for molesting his step-daughter. Anyway, this is a little fresh for me because my mother is older now. And [name omitted] and three of his brothers were coming to do something in the area close to where my mother lives. They are coming to pick up a car or something. And they are coming into the house to stay the night and visit my mom and them. And I told my mother I wouldn't be there. And she begged me to stay. And I told her I couldn't stay. I reminded her. This is not a good place for me. Not because at the time I was very emotional about it. [It's] Just not a good choice for me. And she said, "Well, what about forgiveness?" [She said] "But, I need you here." And so right now I'm kind of stuck in that place. That this is bigger than it was before. I'm kind of stuck in that place. Okay, yeah, I was three and I don't think of it. I don't really consider that a lot of my life is around this particular incident. However, I'm just not feeling all warm and family feelings here. Yet, my mother does need help with people visiting. And she does need help around just having a lot of people in the house. And then what about forgiveness and what does that really mean for me? Yeah.

Tamara felt stuck in a difficult position, but her ambivalence yielded to self-preservation. While acknowledging the difficult demands her mother's pleas for forgiveness placed on her, Tamara prioritized the importance of her own emotional (and perhaps physical or sexual) safety. She decided that her spiritual well-being necessitated that she not place herself back in her abuser's presence, or forgive her cousin who had not owned up to any wrongdoing. This was not an easy decision for Tamara, and it was one she faced multiple times as she dealt with pressure from her family to forgive her cousin and simply move along.

Decisions like the one Tamara faced, and the questions they asked of themselves, God, and others led them to various conclusions about justice and violence. Informed by the spiritual views and wisdom they had developed about their cultural surroundings, each of them came to various interpretations of what violence meant for their personal identity and relationship with God. They arrived at these conclusions through questioning God's absence and/or presence at the time of their violation; through looking at the pain for what it taught them about themselves; and looking at the pain for what it taught them about sins against women in a culture that condones their violation.

Cirene questioned God's absence and/or presence at the time of the violence as well as at other points of turmoil that continued long after her cousin's incestuous abuse ended:

> *Cirene*: I struggle with God not being there, or God not changing what happened. That's [what] my theology really says, and even as a child my theology was "God is in control. Period." And so, God is so high and mighty and in control, how come God didn't stop this? And so I also think there's a reason, a purpose. Could I have been me without it?
>
> *Stephanie*: Could I have been me without it?
>
> *Cirene*: Yeah. Could I still have the same thoughts, could I still have the same compassion, could I just you know be analytical without this incident? And was it so essential to my being now, or should I even spend time doing all that, 'cause it is what it is? So I've always struggled with that whole thing. But even through the midst of the journey, I always call God someone who really has sustained my mind, because even when I started taking Ecstasy and stuff like that, I was really just drifting away. But church really pulled me back. A lot of things I wouldn't do, a lot of things I haven't done, because of my call. And I've done a lot, but some of the things that I just...I just have to explore on the sides. That's what we are...explorers by nature. And, so a lot of the things that I would have done...But my call—that image around my call—however helpful or harmful it is, it's still an image in my head, and a lot of the things I haven't done because of it. Because of this kind of sense of God in my life, so that's some of the things that I think I—I'm not struggling with it

so much as to why. My thing is how do I use it to help other people, or how do I use it even in my journey now to help myself, or how can I pull from it. But before, I just couldn't understand why—why did that have to happen for me to end up here?

Cirene believed that where she presently found herself was good in terms of her work in the ministry and her work with other women who have experienced violence. Arrival at this point, however, was not easy. She struggled with God's absence and/or presence at the time of abuse, while maintaining belief in God because God was a sustaining presence when she was self-mutilating (cutting), abusing drugs and alcohol, and other risky behaviors she used to cope with the effects of years of incestuous abuse. For Cirene, the call to minister to others who similarly suffered the defilement of abuse was proof that God had a plan for her life that included both the pain she had experienced and the wisdom on healing that she had gained. A crucial element of this work and healing had to do with how working to raise awareness and end intimate violence helped her resist cultural and religious pressure to simply move along quietly.

Rori's strategy for making meaning of the violence she experienced was to focus on the various life lessons she learned from surviving childhood rape and repeated intimate violence in adulthood. When she thought back through her experiences with drug and alcohol abuse and sexual risk taking, she viewed them like chapters in a book that taught her about her strengths, weaknesses, and even God:

You know, I don't know, I guess, as old folks say, I've been "in the way" long enough to know. It's supposed to be *on* the way, but I've been *in* the way long enough. *In* the way long enough to know that some of the choices we make may not send us to whatever they think Hell is. And I always say Hell is any place that's uncomfortable for you. And I've had a lot of Hell in relationships and some other things. But, I've had some heaven in some of those same places, so um, some of the choices would have cause. And I always wonder, I always ask myself, if I could change certain things, would I? But, then I know that if I change anything that whole cycle would be messed up. So, I just say, well let me try to learn from what I already experienced so I won't have to keep going through that circle again and again and again. But, it seems that it may...It's not going through the same, but you are still going through the circle.

Rori's spiritual journey involved reinterpreting the religious language handed to her. Rather than heeding the church's teaching that it is "bad" to be *on* the way, she refashioned the language to speak of how she exercised choice to be "in the way." For her, not only being "in" the way but openly owning the choices she made led her to the conclusion that painful life experiences presented her with opportunities to know herself and God more deeply.

Both Rori and Octavia's interrogation of their circumstances led them to conclude that intimate violence was a rite of passage that facilitated their awareness of how treacherous life for girls and women can be:

> *Rori*: I'm always telling my story. But, the idea of being able to help someone else overcome or realize that there's some things that all women go through. It's almost like a rite of passage now. And there are different forms of rites of passage. And either way you always come out better than you were before.
>
> *Octavia*: It seems like most men, and even when I was in college doing student teaching it didn't matter. It seemed like a lot of the relationships that I had with men they always wanted something. That's why when I was assaulted it seemed like, okay, this is kind of like everything that's happened took me to this point....And it [group counseling] really gave me a sense of knowing that I'm not alone. That these things, maybe they are, in a sense, a rite of passage. Maybe not this extreme, but, you have to go through some things in order to know just how to be. How to be. How to get through. How to get over. How to just be.

For Octavia the violent initiation of rape was part of developing a spiritual strength and worldview that would prepare her to face life. When she reflected back on her experience, she took note of the many women she personally knew, as well as many others, who had experienced sexual violence.

She, as well as Cirene, Rori, and Eliza all arrived at the conclusion that not only experiencing but also surviving and "living to tell the story" of overcoming allowed them to move forward in their relationship with God. "Living to tell the story" was a hugely significant aspect of the meaning they made of violence they experienced. They were able to integrate defiling experiences of violence into their commitments about God's divine purpose for their lives because they found ways to draw spiritual strength and wisdom from their struggles. This allowed them to see their pain as a part, not the whole, of their experience. Struggling with God, self, and community over their hurts prepared them to acknowledge others' pain and to witness how God responds to this pain by extending a sustaining presence. This outlook was grounded in their belief that the spiritual strength and practical wisdom they had developed was not for their use alone, but rather for the betterment of the community. All of the women expressed this as part of their reason for participating in the research for this book.

The reconstructed spirituality that emerged as a result of their interrogation and audacity to embody a relationship with God grounded the women. The resistant, interrogative nature of their faith sustained them when they struggled with matters of justice, forgiveness, shame, and pain. Theirs was a salvific connection with God. But, what about the church's role in their healing? While the women interrogated the church, none of them walked away from it never to return. As a matter of fact, many were actively involved in the church, though on their own terms. These women's realities raise an important tension for the church, especially concerning its underlying commitments around embodiment, pain and suffering—themes that sit at the center of its traditions around views of the incarnation and atonement. Womanist theologians Kelly Brown Douglas's and Delores S. Williams's analysis illuminates how classic views of the incarnation and the atonement fuel the very views of the body and suffering that the women interrogated in the process of reconstructing a spirituality kept them connected to a God they could recognize.

In *Sexuality and the Black Church: A Womanist Perspective,*[5] Douglas sorts through the implications of disembodied views of the incarnation for how Black people (including women) make meaning in their lives based on their interpretation of God's incarnation in the historical Jesus. In contrast to disembodied views of the incarnation, in which Jesus' enfleshed experienced is inconsequential to God's work, embodied views of the incarnation affirm God's affinity for embodied experience—the flesh. Interpretive traditions based on disembodied views of the incarnation presume that the flesh is the cause of creation's existential separation from God. This perspective informs the theological position that sin is ontological, "whereby the fault or flaw is in [human] existence"[6] itself. Translation: Bodies are sinfully problematic.

To be clear, the tension over how to acknowledge the incarnation as an affirmation of the flesh as ontologically "good" exists across racial and ethnic lines within Christianity. However, the legacy of legally sanctioned physical and sexual assault during chattel slavery, and in the subsequent Antebellum, Jim and Jane Crow, and Civil Rights eras tempers Black women and men's embrace of this ontological truth in a particularly racialized way. The desire is present, but generations of internalized racial and sexual oppression make the embrace both complicated and awkward. These historic experiences, coupled with classic disembodied views of the incarnation that deemphasize Jesus's physicality as inconsequential to God's saving work, have had the effect of inculcating fear and anxiety in the relationship that many contemporary Black Christians have with their bodies, inclusive of their sexuality. Overcoming this anxiety to love one's body as the imprint of God's own self is difficult for many Black Christians. The situation is even more complex for Black women whose experience in overcoming barriers to loving themselves wholly also includes religious defamation of their gender and intensely sinful acts of childhood sexual assault, rape, incest, battering, and spiritual abuse. These are the kinds of realities that compel Douglas to declare that Jesus' body did and still does matter:

> The incarnation indicates that God is embodied in human history through Jesus Christ and, as such, is an intimately active presence in the lives of women and men. A sexual discourse of resistance seeks to protect this historical realness of God's revelation in Jesus. Such a view demands a theological understanding of the body. It does not compel an idolatrous worship of the body, but it does compel an appreciation of the body as indeed the "very temple of God," as the medium of God's love. It is by becoming embodied that God was distinctly revealed in human history; moreover, it is only via bodies that human beings can come to know and be in relationship with one another. We reach out to one another with our bodies, and we accept one another as embodied.[7]

Douglas's theologizing helps us see the implications of an embodied view of the incarnation on our capacity to extend ourselves and receive one another as witnesses of God's presence in the world. Even still, disembodied views of the incarnation are prominent fixtures in contemporary congregations. Williams reminds us, "More often than not the theology in mainline Protestant churches (including African American ones) teaches believers that sinful humankind has been redeemed because Jesus died on the cross in the place of humans, thereby taking human sin upon himself."[8] The concomitant claim that bodies are ontologically sinful undergirds this view. According to this tradition, crucifixion of the Christ's flesh was the only way to redeem humanity from its ontological sinfulness, which subsequently resulted in classic dualist claims that the flesh (the body and its vicissitudes) is something to distrust because it is inherently antagonistic to God's will. A consequence of this view for Christians in general is that it makes it very easy to overlook pain and suffering that bodies endure. The struggle to claim their flesh as ontologically good is even more difficult for Christians whose bodies have been systemically subjugated and made to suffer simply because of the color, gender, and sexual orientation of their flesh.

Williams's embodied views of the incarnation are helpful in addressing this tension because they dislocate sin away from an ontological origin to locate it in structures that ravish, violate, sully, and dishonor (defile) human lives.[9] An embodied view of the incarnation, combined with an understanding of sin as structural rather than ontological, positions us to see more clearly the correlation between Black women's ability to reclaim themselves and God and the social and religious practices that frustrate these important, intimate connections. flesh (the body and its vicissitudes).[10]

Williams's critique of classic theories of atonement advances Douglas's work by situating Black women's traumatic experience in an incarnational theology, which prompts further interrogation of whether Black women may be saved through suffering, like Jesus:

> For Black women, there is also the question of whether Jesus on the cross represents coerced surrogacy (willed by the Father) or voluntary surrogacy (chosen by the son) or both. At any rate, a major theological problem here is the place of the cross in any theology significantly informed by African-American women's experience with surrogacy. Even if one buys into the notion of the cross as the meeting place of the will of God to give up the Son (coerced surrogacy) and the will of the Son to give up himself (voluntary surrogacy?) so that "the spirit of abandonment and self-giving love" proceeds from the cross to "raise up abandoned men," African American women are still left with the question: Can there be salvific power for Black women in Christian images of oppression (for example Jesus on the cross) meant to teach something about redemption?[11]

Williams is primarily concerned with making theological space to claim lived realities of (en)forced oppression and suffering as the point of departure for questioning the validity of classic views of atonement when one has been systemically made to sacrifice one's body for others. Williams identifies Black women's experiences of enslavement and domestic servitude as the particular point of departure. To that, I also add childhood sexual assault, incest, molestation, rape, and battering (much of which also occurred in addition to and in the contexts of the experience of enslavement and domestic service), wherein Black women's bodies are made to service the malicious objectification of those who abuse them.

Douglas's and Williams's analysis and critique inform a hermeneutic lens for examining church traditions that significantly impact how Black women views themselves as bearing the image of God, and efforts to reclaim their bodies, sensuality, and sexualities from intimate and cultural violence. This hermeneutic supports a listening stance that emphasizes recognition and appreciation of the ways in which women engage faith as a personal, spiritual, and cultural practice of resistance and as a source of fulfilment.

Developing a hermeneutic based on analysis of key Christian traditions is a necessary first step in the theological work that has to be done in order to hear fully Black women's stories. However, Womanist work is about more than developing ways to hear. It's about contributing ideas on how to actively respond to what we hear in ways that resonate with the lives of those we serve. How do we bring these women's narratives into conversation with Womanist analysis? Secondarily, what are the implications of bringing these two bodies of knowledge (everyday Black women and Womanist analysis) to bear upon pastoral theology's discourse? Finally, what does it look like to translate this dialogue into meaningful engagement on the ground? I engage these questions in the following two chapters on Womanist pastoral care and Womanist pastoral counseling.

4

WomanistCare: Reshaping Images and Paradigms for Care

Pastoral response that resonates with the ways Black women approach self-recovery and healing requires new images and paradigms for care. I respond to this need in this chapter by introducing *working images of WomanistCare* that prompt pastoral theological reflection on practitioners' cultural countertransference responses to Black women and existing norms for care. Next, a case study of WomanistCare ritual is presented for analysis and reflection on ritual as a congregation-based, communal act of care. The analysis includes discussion of the use and abuse of power in ritual space convened to meet the needs of women who have experienced violence.

A review of how the women I interviewed met their needs for emotional, physical, social, and spiritual support revealed that only a few of them turned to the institutions of formal psychotherapy and counseling. Although they struggled with the church as an institution, they never altogether abandoned it as an important cultural selfobject and space for community. Instead of approaching psychotherapists and counselors, they acted as agents in their own healing and drew on everyday relationships and encounters to help them navigate intimate and cultural violence without giving up their voice or humanity. These uninstitutionalized experiences included:

- encounters with OtherMothers and Sisterfriends whose practical support and alternative insights on intimate and cultural violence mirrored their humanity and firmed up their interior experience of self

- female cultural selfobjects, who, through acts of service, civic office and performance on public platforms offered uplifting visual images and spiritual insight that empowered them to survive, heal, and resist a culture that normalizes violence against them
- examination of the impact of religious messages that mediate or mitigate cultural violence through misogynistic/patriarchal gender norms in their relationships with God, self, and others
- reconstructing a spirituality that honors the particularities of their personal experience, integrates non-Christian religious traditions, and offers theological language that mirrors back the fullness of their distinctly female humanity (inclusive of their bodies) as a reflection of God's femininity
- embodied spiritual practices that simultaneously connected them to God while also functioning as a strategy for interrupting unwanted cultural access to their bodies and ethnic identities
- transforming the position that trauma holds in their lives by using personal experiences and stories of overcoming to help other women who have similarly struggled with intimate violence.

Constructing an empowering congregational response to violence begins with taking these experiences seriously as the meter against which the norms embedded in caring responses made available to Black women are assessed. We begin this assessment by examining the root metaphors and classic images of care circulating in pastoral theology's discourse. Womanist pastoral theologian Marsha Foster Boyd explains,

In developing a pastoral theology one must examine the traditional images and roles used in describing those giving and receiving care within the context of the church. Traditionally, the images of the pastor as "shepherd" and the parishioners as "flock" are predominant. WomanistCare is a response to this form of pastoral theology that is predominately white, male, linear, and fraternal, and that traditionally lifts up such images of shepherd and servant as the primary means by which care is given and received.[1]

Womanist pastoral theologian Carroll Watkins Ali also critiques the shepherding paradigm for its inadequacy in helping
practitioners address the survival and liberation dimensions of
many African Americans' pastoral concerns:

> Together Black theology and Black psychology reveal that the
> experience of the African American context calls for staffs of
> ministers in every church who are preachers, teachers and pas-
> toral psychotherapists, too, if African Americans are to survive
> and become free from their oppressions, both spiritually and
> psychologically. In terms of the existential concerns that are
> material and encompass the *survival of all the people* as well as
> liberation from oppression, congregations must become part of
> larger ecumenical systems and networks that advocate for issues
> that are socioeconomic and political in nature.[2]

Watkins Ali argues for a definition of pastoral care providers as advocates who connect individuals with others (social
service providers, advocacy groups, counselors, employers)
and who can address parishioners' survival needs.[3] Like Foster
Boyd, Watkins Ali also critiques pastoral theology's wide acceptance of the power dynamic that is inherent in the shepherding
paradigm,[4] which privileges the caregiver's personal and professional experience as the authoritative source for understanding
the life experience of the person who seeks care. Both suggest
that this power paradigm further disempowers people whose
cultural experience is often one of having their self-knowledge
invalidated by others in positions of power.

Watkins Ali's and Foster Boyd's relational, cultural, and theological critiques are part of a growing collective of voices who are
attuned to the need for a shift in discourse concerning care with
Black women.[5] I agree with their analyses. However, in light of
how race, gender, culture, sexuality, and class converged to create matrixes of power in the lives of the women I interviewed,
I find it necessary to extend their critiques. Watkins Ali's critique does not speak as clearly as I would like to the importance of practitioners' self-awareness of their own experience
of images, institutions, symbols, and relational paradigms that

negatively impact Black women. Also, the writings of both these women stop short of concretizing their proposed paradigms in an example of care in action, upon which practitioners could project their ideas about Black women's interiority and social location, and subsequently engage in critical reflection on the implications of these projections for when they approach care and counseling with Black women. I am additionally interested in identifying resources that help us cast our nets more widely in the search for images and narratives that instruct the discipline on what communal care looks like, and how to go about engaging the community in tending to Black female selves.

A Working Image of WomanistCare

I pick up where Foster Boyd and Watkins Ali left off to pursue the notion of a *working image of WomanistCare*—an enfleshed image of pastoral care that represents the sociohistoric experience of Black women's experience in culture and the methods that help them thrive in spite of that culture. I do so to offer an appropriate image of care that matches the vicissitudes of care with African American women; that supports practitioners' ongoing development of selfawareness of their cultural countertransference with Black females; and to excavate resources that stress the importance of including the articulation of how structural oppression impacts Black bodies in communal healing practices. By "cultural countertransference" I mean the deeply held, unconsciously motivated leanings about race, sexuality, class, ethnicity, gender, and various other physical markers of social location that often result in stereotypes about Black women.[6] The "working" part of the term intends to suggest that the cultural countertransference that emerges in response to Black female bodies, sexualities, and identities is dynamic. It is an intersubjective reality that requires ongoing work to develop the kind of self-awareness and internal reflection that positions practitioners to be co-laborers in Black women's liberation, truthtelling, empowerment, and healing.

Through depictions of Black women's interior experience, working images of WomanistCare place before practitioners the racial, economic, gendered, and sexual oppression that can frame women's identities, while demonstrating care that responds to this oppression. As heuristic devices, they prompt pastoral theological reflection on (1) the practitioners' own experience of (and/or complicity in) historic and contemporary practices that negatively distort Black female selves; (2) subsequent assumptions about Black women's interior experience of God, self, and others; and (3) care that resonates with Black women's psychological, cultural, and spiritual strategies for self-recovery and healing. As a consequence, they offer access to Black interiority in ways that illuminate and name sources and dynamics of oppression. Secondarily, critical reflection on working images of WomanistCare creates time and space for care providers to consider healing from complicity in and/or experiences of intimate and cultural violence. This, in turn, strengthens and grounds the self and space that pastoral practitioners make available to Black women.

Much of what I am calling for in a working image of WomanistCare is conjured and imaginatively captured in characters like Toni Morrison's, "Baby Suggs, holy" from the novel, *Beloved*.[7] In Baby Suggs, holy we find an enfleshed image of care that embodies the predicaments of racial, economic, sexual, emotional, and physical violence. Morrison also uses this character to suggest a paradigm for care that responds to these violences. My use of Morrison's Baby Suggs, holy situates me within a Black[8] and Womanist[9] theological tradition of engaging Black literature as doorways to African American interiority. Particular to Womanist pastoral theology, Sheppard and Watkins Ali have both suggested the work of Toni Morrison, Alice Walker, Zora Neale Hurston, and others as critical texts that explore Black women's interior experience of culture, self, and others. I engage Morrison's work in this manner but go a step further by inviting pastoral practitioners to reflect on Morrison's character as a doorway for examining unnamed social and cultural biases within themselves, as well as within the norms in the discipline that inform expectations of what practices of care in congregational settings look like.

In using Morrison's work this way, I am critiquing classic paradigms in the field that traditionally offer images of care (the counselor, the clown, the rebel, the advocate in the human web, the gardener)[10] without locating that image in the physicality of a particular social and historical context. Contemporary pastoral theologians have been hard at work addressing this gap in the literature,[11] and I attribute the gap to a well-intentioned effort on the part of theorists to avoid the trap of universalizing experience. But, when we fail to hold before us modes of care that are enfleshed in the physicality of a particular social location, do we not skip over the tension that emerges concerning the normativity of some social locations and the marginalization of others? Bodies and social identities matter. They are part of the cultural countertransference that speaks to how we view ourselves and how we act in relation to others. Focusing on this particularity comes with hazards of its own. We have to approach the ongoing work of developing self-awareness of cultural countertransference (our unconsciously motivated leanings about race, class, gender, sexuality, ethnicity, and other aspects of embodiment) without treating those who seek care like objects who meet the needs of our educational development. Training programs like Clinical Pastoral Education (CPE) and counseling practicums are certainly good supports for this work. However, not even even these carefully structured learning spaces are exempt from being significantly influenced by cultural stereotypes.[12] Secondarily, many African American women experience these contexts as unsafe for their own development when non-Black colleagues often turn to them as teachers on Black experience at a time in their learning when they themselves are struggling to develop self-awareness around tensions in their own experience as Black women. That having been said, I do not knock CPE and counseling practicums. I affirm and endorse them as good and necessary training processes. I am, however, arguing for Black literature as a resource that supplements practitioners' efforts to go deeper.

Black literature offers us a tool for cultivating self-awareness of cultural countertransference with Black women, without requiring that Black women take up the role of teaching (giving of themselves) in circumstances when they themselves are in need of care. This is my concern regarding developing the skills and disposition that is helpful in doing care with African American women, but I would argue that similar moves need to be made to excavate images of care that are grounded in the physicality of various communities that have experienced social, ethnic, and cultural marginalization. Below, I engage Baby Suggs, holy to demonstrate how Morrison's character offers a tool for examining cultural countertransference norms that inform how we can respond pastorally to intimate and cultural violence.

Cultural Countertransference and Black Female Bodies

In *Beloved,* Morrison depicts Baby Suggs, holy as an elder ex-slave who is able to make her home on the other side of the Ohio River because her son bought her freedom. Now free, she brings forth life out of the death-dealing circumstances she endured as an enslaved African American woman. Morrison describes her as a woman "who decided that, because slave life had 'busted her legs, back, head, eyes, hands, kidneys, womb and tongue,' she had nothing left to make a living with but her heart—which she put to work at once."[13] Her home provides communal respite for Blacks, some of whom are free as well as for those on the run for their freedom. These people include her daughter-in-law, Sethe, who arrives on her doorstep with a newborn in tow after she had escaped white male owners who beat and raped her while she was pregnant. This home is also where, acting in the role of OtherMother, Baby Suggs, holy nurses Sethe back to sanity after Sethe kills her newborn daughter and attempts to do the same with her other children rather than allow bountyhunters to take them back to the plantation they escaped.

A key moment for pastoral practitioners reading the text is the scene where Baby Suggs, holy calls the community to gather, to come heal from Sethe and everyone else's pain together. Fully aware of the evils of American enslavement, Baby Suggs, holy calls women, men, and children who had been beaten, raped, and assaulted to come worship in secret, out in the woods. There, in a clearing, she invites them to remember the basics of their humanity (joy, desire, sadness, freedom). She commands them to dance, laugh, and weep in spite of their circumstances. When they respond they find themselves safely re-bodied and open to what the Spirit has to say about their humanity through her. She responds with a sermon that clearly names racism and patriarchy that wound the spirits of her community, while also offering a space to practice embodied spiritual resistance:

"Let the children come!" and they ran from the trees toward her. "Let your mothers hear you laugh," she told them, and the woods rang. The adults looked on and could not help smiling. Then "Let the grown men come," she shouted. They stepped out one by one from among the ringing trees. "Let your wives and your children see you dance," she told them, and ground life shuddered under their feet. Finally she called the women to her. "Cry," she told them. "For the living and the dead. Just cry." And without covering their eyes the women let loose. It started that way: laughing children, dancing men, crying women and then it got mixed up. Women stopped crying and danced; men sat down and cried; children danced, women laughed, children cried until, exhausted and riven all and each lay about the Clearing damp and gasping for breath. In the silence that followed, Baby Suggs, offered up to them her great big heart...

"Here in this place, we flesh; flesh that weeps, laughs; flesh that dances on bare feet in grass. Love it. Love it hard. Yonder, they do not love your flesh. They despise it. They don't love your eyes; they'd just as soon pick them out. No more do they love the skin on your back. Yonder they flay it. And oh, my people they do not love your hands. Those they only use, tie, bind, chop off, and leave empty. Love your hands! Love them. Raise them up and kiss them. Touch others with them, pat them together, stroke them on your face cause they don't love that either. *You* got to love it, you! An no, they ain't in love with your mouth. Yonder, out there, they will see it broken and break it again. What you say out of it they will not heed. What you scream from it they do not hear. What you put into it to nourish your body they will snatch away and give you leavins instead. No, they don't love your mouth. *You* got to love it. This is flesh I'm talking about here. Flesh that needs to be loved. Feet that need to rest and to dance; backs that need support; shoulders that need arms, strong arms I'm telling you. And Oh my people, out yonder, hear me they do not love your neck un-noosed and straight. So love your neck; put a hand on it, grace it, stroke it and hold it up. And all your inside parts that they'd just a soon have as slop for hogs, you got to love them. The dark, dark liver—love it, love it, and the beat and beating heart, love that too. More than eyes or feet. More than lungs that have yet to draw free air. More than your life-holding women and your life-giving private parts, hear me now, love your heart. For this is the prize."[14]

Morrison's character is fictitious, yet the truth is that Baby Suggs, holy provides important clues on what has traditionally healed Black minds, bodies, and souls in America. Morrison crafts this scene of Baby Suggs, holy convening an outdoor worship experience based on historic accounts of enslaved Africans who secretly withdrew to the woods where they could worship God in ways that were authentic to their spirituality, and completely apart from the ways they were forced to worship in Christian churches under the watchful eye of slave-owners. The work taps into the historic legacy of faith as a critical ingredient in an African American spirituality of resistance.[15] Her imaginative depiction conjures the collective memory of enslaved and freed elders who nurtured themselves and others through acts of hospitality in inhumane contexts, through healing touch in times of torture, and through an embodied spiritualty that empowered them to resist the evils of physical, psychological, sexual, and spiritual bondage.

Baby Suggs, holy highlights the prophetic role of African American writers. Through her, Morrison perpetuates the legacy of Black female writers who do the work of recalling memories of people and lives that affirmed life in the face of death-dealing circumstances.[16]

Their recall offers important information on how Black people hurt, what hurts them, and how to actively speak against these physical, sexual, emotional and political ailments. It is important to acknowledge, however, that these characters come to the page bearing more than historic memories. Baby Suggs, holy is an amalgam of history and hope. Her sermon in the clearing directs readers on how to name, disrupt, and become free from the spiritual bondage of violence. Her ethic of care embodies many African Americans' hopes for holistic pastoral care that is salvific for the mind, body, and soul. As a writer, Morrison has the benefit of hindsight as the lens through which she looks back at African American memories of race trauma. From the vantage point of being born in 1931, she recalls the healing ways of these elders, but she adds to their experience by filling in the blanks with her awareness of what else contemporary African Americans may need in order to heal. By speaking of intimate wounds that have often been "too terrible to relate,"[17] she reminds and instructs contemporary readers of how formerly enslaved African American ancestors talked back to the systems that bust, wound, and kill bodies and souls. It is Morrison's lesson to remember so that we can survive now. Although fictitious, Baby Suggs, holy is true, and the historic healing legacy that Morrison depicts through her resonates with the experiences, images, and encounters that helped the women I interviewed develop salvific relationships with themselves and others.

Black literature like this is valuable because it is instructive and intentional. It draws on historic memory of what has plagued African Americans. When pastoral scholars and practitioners engage this re-presentation of embodied Black female history they are also confronted with a narrative that sits in the historical background of the cultural countertransference that emerges in response to Black female bodies and identities. The significance of this historic representation of an elder, Black, holy woman resisting the effects of oppression is that it enfleshes a narrative that instructs what it looks like to grapple seriously with the multiple facets of violence committed against Black women.

Unlike the defiling cultural representations that demean Black womanhood (Mammy, Sapphire, Jezebel, and their derivatives), Baby Suggs, holy embodies a Womanist ethic of care that names and confronts how cultural and intimate violence damage bodies, psyches, and souls. She is especially concerned with addressing her communities' internalization of white hatred for Black flesh, which she addresses by admonishing them to "love it, love it hard" because over "yonder" they do not.

To make oneself wholly available to this image of care that is grounded in Black women's physical, social, and historic experience is to allow oneself the opportunity to name and reflect on the impact that racism and various forms of violence have had on all minds and bodies. In clinical supervision and pastoral theological discourse scholars and practitioners must grapple not only with working images of WomanistCare, but also with how we internalize, reject, or stand in ambiguity with the historical narratives of institutionalized violence and oppression that the images recall. The concreteness of Morrison's depiction of Baby Suggs, holy's busted body clarifies how sinful sociopolitical systems in the American context have impacted Black female bodies, minds, and spirits and shaped cultural attitudes and projections about them.

This awareness is important not just for Black women pastoral theologians and practitioners, but for anyone (all of us) working with Black women whose self-development in a historical context includes a legacy of bodies and spirits busted by institutionalized poverty, racism, and gendered violence. This working image of WomanistCare and resistance offers pastoral theology a resource that empowers practitioners to develop cultural empathy and self-awareness regarding race, class, gender, and sexuality. This image directs practitioners' attention to parts of themselves that have been "busted" by systemic sin—including those who are inevitably wounded in the process of oppressing others. If taken seriously, practitioners find a resource that names evil forces at play in society, while also being confronted with realities that force them to consider how they may benefit from and/or find themselves complicit in these same forces.

Reflecting on working images of WomanistCare depicted in Black literature that emerge out of the particularity of Black women's historical and cultural experience is important. They allow a level of distance between practitioners and actual Black women that allows them to go deep into oftentimes disavowed beliefs about Black girls and women without requiring that Black girls and women subject themselves to these projections while practitioners develop the kind of self-awareness that is capable of supporting true healing. It creates a safe (for Black women seeking support, as well as for the practitioner) space to examine the stereotypes, social norms and historical experiences that are directly and indirectly part of the social context within which Black women live and develop. However, neither safe reflection on literature, nor self-awareness are enough. We must keep this insight in dialogue with the lived experience and insight of women like the ones whose voices we've heard in the previous chapters. Of all the things that stood out in their narratives, some form of embodied practice and ritual was one of the most critical aspects of their healing journey. Below I consider what insights from their stories, in conjunction with Morrison's carefully authored depiction of healing through ritual, have to offer concerning the community's role in supporting Black women's health and healing.

Healing Through Communal Ritual

Cultivating therapeutic space for Black women to experience care and affirmation requires that pastoral theology continually assess the tools at its disposal—including exploring if and how the norms guiding pastoral praxis accommodate the diverse ways that Black women communicate with themselves, others, and God. Marsha Foster Boyd points out that healing for Black women includes communicating stories and feelings "through various mediums including visual and performing arts, craft making and sacred rituals."[18] Research with the women I interviewed confirmed this. They used writing, dancing, sewing, singing, and meditation as embodied spiritual practices that supported this communication.

Foster Boyd points out that a key aspect of their efficacy was that they circumvented social, cultural, and economic barriers that sometimes prevent traditional psychotherapy from being a desirable or viable context of care for many Black women. Foster Boyd explains, "Since there is sometimes mistrust of the traditional counseling model, WomanistCare works to transcend its potential limitations among African Americans, regardless of class."[19] What are those limitations? Historically, psychological theory has pathologized African Americans and justified their disenfranchisement. Its typically hegemonic norms often do not acknowledge the multiple, uninstitutionalized ways that Black women like the ones whose voices we heard in the previous chapters approach healing. While I affirm the usefulness of psychotherapy (when adjusted to address cultural norms in Black women's lives), I am equally interested in pursuing Black women's uninstitutionalized strategies as a guide for Womanist pastoral support. The embodied practices of the women I interviewed indicated the need for ritual, where they could claim their truths, and for a safe space in which their bodies might also speak.

Pastoral theological reflection on the role of ritual in the lives of these women prompts me to consider how organizing communal rituals for women in congregational settings might likewise offer safe and affirming voices, space, symbols, and images that maintain life-giving connections with God, self, and others. By ritual I mean to speak of the "ancient way of binding a community together in a close relationship with Spirit."[20] By "Spirit" I am referring to God as the Supreme Being and Ultimate Reality, the existential presence and activity of Jesus, the Holy Spirit, and ancestors from one's cultural and familial lineage.[21] Through symbols and language, ritual acknowledges (without attempting to specifically define) "important occurrences, while pointing to transition and future change."[22] These occurrences may be related to normal life-cycle transitions (naming ceremonies for infants, marriages, deaths) or traumatic transitions that are often invisible and unrecognized. Concerning Black women's experiences of intimate and cultural violence, rituals provide a method and practice for bringing the individual and community together to acknowledge the unrecognized traumatic transitions that occur in women's faith lives as a result of childhood sexual assault, molestation, incest, rape, battering, and other forms of abuse.

Like Baby Suggs, holy's gathering in the clearing, contemporary WomanistCare ritual gatherings invite women into a sacred space that facilitates healing. Through it, the community sees, hears, bears witness to, and participates in God's contact with

Black women and the narratives they bring to the space. Below I offer a brief vignette detailing a ritual practiced by women of various ages at the First Afrikan Presbyterian church in Lithonia, Georgia, as an entry point to consider what a woman-centered communal ritual may have to offer in support of congregation-based care. Although the invitation to the community did not specifically indicate this as a ritual to acknowledge intimate violence, the female-centered orientation, intergenerational context, culturally sensitive theological language, and embodied practices involved in this gathering provide a solid foundation for conceptualizing ritual space that is dedicated to addressing intimate and cultural violence. I conclude with a discussion of clinical concerns for offering ritual as a space for sacred healing in the lives of women who have particular vulnerabilities stemming from previous abuses of power.

First Afrikan Presbyterian Church in Lithonia is an Afrocentric congregation that describes itself as a

> ...Re-formation of Christian ministry in the United States of America. We bear witness to God and the Christ of God in full recognition of the legacy left to us by our Ancestors who, despite the holocausts of enslavement and colonization, forged new identities that gave their progeny both in the motherland and in the diaspora, new life, new hope, and new meaning. We can therefore say that we are not ashamed of the Gospel of Jesus the Christ. It is the power of God for the salvation of Afrikans as well as other peoples on the planet.[23]

Part of this re-formation and commitment involves unashamedly claiming and working to fully integrate African communal and religious traditions into the congregation's interpretations of Christianity. This particular cultural and religious stance demonstrates the congregation's awareness of how cultural violence negatively affects African American women, men, boys, and girls. The "Eight Bowls" ritual described below is an example of this church's commitment to reclaiming African spirituality as a resource for African American survival and self-recovery, especially for women.

On August 29, 2010, the women's ministry and the department of Christian education at First Afrikan Presbyterian church hosted a WomanistCare ritual. The purpose of the ritual was to offer women from the church and surrounding community a sacred space in which to gather and collectively acknowledge each other's experience of life exploration, challenge, transition, triumph, and transformation. The outdoor ritual space consisted of chairs and tables arranged in a large circle. Itihari Toure,[24] minister of Christian Education and ordained elder at First Afrikan Presbyterian Church, opened the ceremony with a prayer and libations, in which water was poured on the earth to recall the legacy of significant female family members and historical Black women. As Toure poured the water, women were invited to call out the names of ancestors—important women who had died and physically transitioned, but whose spiritual presence remain very much present among the women. These ancestors were blood relatives (mothers, grandmothers, aunts, cousins); fictive kin (OtherMothers and Sisterfriends); or Black female cultural selfobjects and sheroes (Audre Lorde, Sojourner Truth, Nina Simone, and many others). After each ancestor's name was called, the community responded, "Ase'"[25] to acknowledge the ancestors' spiritual presence in the gathered space. Next, Ifa[26] priestess Eniola Kalimara invited the women to prepare themselves for the ritual by removing their shoes and cleansing their hands, head, and feet in water infused with rosemary and lavender. She explained that these herbs are specifically used to detoxify the mind, body, and spirit of disruptive energy.

Following the cleansing, the women were grouped by decade beginning with age twenty, and invited to come to the center of the circle. As each group came forward, a woman from the previous group, who had just passed the age of the concerned group, was assigned the task of looking back to offer words of wisdom about what she had learned during that particular season of life. Each such woman offered wisdom, blessings, and affirmations of women's inherent value, as well as the admonition to claim a purpose for their lives regardless of encounters with adversity.

The intent was to acknowledge experiences that challenged the force of life within them, while also reminding the women that although there may have been significant pain and loss, they had persevered and survived. When women of each age group came forward, they were invited to taste the following elements that symbolically represented the vicissitudes of life and the multiplicity of experience in women's lives: wine, honey, lime, salt, cayenne pepper, water, palm oil, and coconut. As bowls containing each element were passed around, the woman offering the blessing explained that each element represented spiritual and ethical principles that have provided, and would continue to provide, resources for interpreting life and grappling with adversity at various seasons in each woman's life:

> *Wine.* It represents appreciation for tradition and family. As well, wine symbolizes strength in racial/ethnic pride, commitment to household and extended family, and reverence and appreciation for the foundation laid by those who came before.
>
> *Honey.* It represents an ability to appreciate and remember the sweetness and goodness of life.
>
> *Lime.* It represents an ability to overcome bitterness by retaining dignity, composure, and self-worth, even when feeling hurt by words, actions, or inaction of others.
>
> *Salt.* It symbolizes wisdom and balance in making life choices as well as flexibility, creativity, variety, and moral balance.
>
> *Cayenne pepper.* It represents resilience in response to critical situations and reminds participants to expect unpredictable circumstances and to develop the ability to rebound in the face of crisis.
>
> *Water.* The fluid of life represents a willingness to change. Additionally, water represents spiritual depth and renewal and coolness in the midst of crises.
>
> *Palm oil.* It represents reliance on community power. More essentially, the palm oil represents an ability to move towards inevitable death with confidence and grace. This confidence can be born of a cohesive family and community where each person is valued for their contribution.
>
> *Coconut.* Fresh, broken coconut symbolizes assurance of inevitable blessings and unexpected luck. This coconut also represents

reliance on that which is greater than oneself and life benefits that have nothing to do with an individual's own intelligence, skill, or power, but are due solely to the unpredictable goodness of the divine.[27]

The elements in the bowls correspond with various emotions and seasons of human experience. As each woman tasted the element, she experienced a moment in community in which she could symbolically voice her experience without giving up her privacy or making herself vulnerable to trespasses of her emotional space. Toure notes,

> Only that person knows what particular bitter experience they are addressing. However that taste affects you—it is for *you* to decide your interpretation....It is the community's acknowledgement of the vicissitudes of life. The moment when you taste it, is the space where *you* interpret the meaning.[28]

This interpretive moment happened in community, yet it still respected the privacy of each woman's narrative, memories, and feelings. It also relied on symbols and metaphors to do what language cannot. Jan Berry writes,

> There are some stories that resist telling. Heather Walton argues that some stories cannot be told without domesticating the pain and the horror of experience, and that new ways of speaking need to be found: "What is needed is not narrative but poesis, images, symbols and metaphors that carry the pain of trauma without committing the blasphemy of trying to represent, comprehend or reconcile in story form."[29]

In essence, these symbols, metaphors, and language of the eight-bowl ritual did not make meaning; rather they pointed toward existential realities that offered new possibilities for meaning making.

At the conclusion of the ritual, all of the women who participated were invited to form concentric circles arranged by age. The youngest women were placed at the center and surrounded by the next age group. The eldest women formed the outer ring and offered prayers to bless them along the next season of their lives.

Several points stand out for me as I consider Baby Suggs, holy's gathering in the clearing as a working image of WomanistCare, its parallels with the ritual at First Afrikan, and the implications of both for congregational care with women like the ones I interviewed. I was struck by how the libations called the women to reconnect with female ancestors. I noticed the tone of their voices when they spoke the names of ancestors in their bloodlines, extended family networks, and collective history as African American women. Some spoke loudly and clearly; others' voices were softer and even strained. Some of the names were of women they had never met, but whose songs, writings, artwork, and various other cultural productions had been significant at various seasons in their lives. Some women laughed and smiled as the names left their mouths and entered the atmosphere, while tears veiled other names. The women present weren't just recalling these women's lives; they were recalling encounters and the feelings they held about these ancestral women. They were remembering events, but they were also recalling sights, sounds, smells, and tactile sensations related to these women. They were recalling selfobject experiences in which they felt those women empathically responded to them, or experiences in which their efforts to connect were met with empathically failing responses. Whatever the case, calling these names and their related memories into the space was important to the women who participated, whether those memories were sweet or not.

The ritual made available multiple resources that I believe are helpful in considering a congregation-based ritual for women who experience intimate and cultural violence. The ritual at FAPC affirmed the positive memories and images, but it also made room for contextualizing and grappling with memories of challenging experiences like violence. Through it the congregation's ministry made available intentional symbols, language, images, and embodied practices as resources for making new meaning of difficult experiences that were a part (but not the whole) of who they were. Woman-centered and Africentric, the ritual affirmed women's humanity and ethnic heritage in ways that mitigated the theological and ideological commitments that normalize intimate and cultural violence. Like Baby Suggs, holy's clearing space, this ritual created an opportunity to step off the grid in order to practice what it means to love the Black body...to "love it hard." Communal ritual in a congregational setting like the one above has the capacity to respond to the interests and concerns unearthed in conversations with the women I interviewed. When taken together, each of the elements in the Eight Bowl ritual represents ethical principles that I believe offer helpful language and practices for grappling with the ongoing challenges the women mentioned in interviews.

While such a ritual has the potential to support healing, facilitating a safe therapeutic context for transformation in a congregational context requires clinical awareness of issues of trauma, power, consent, and safety.

Ritual, Power, and Abuse

In the stories of intimate violence that the women shared, the women's use of their own power, as well as how they felt affected by others' use of "power over" (as is the case in abuse), "power within community" (the underlying element in personal and institutional encounters that affirmed their humanity) and "power within" (the interior sense of agency and value that emerged through intimacy with self and God)[30] was a thread that ran through each narrative. For this reason, practitioners must approach ritual space with clinical sensitivity about the use and abuse of power. The following examples of 'power over' in childhood sexual abuse, rape, and battering illuminate the complicated functions of abuse that are often part of the traumatic memories many women carry.

Gail E. Wyatt et al. describe the role of control in the abuse of power ("power over") that takes place in childhood sexual abuse. "The effects of sexual abuse can be long lasting because someone controls: (1) when a victim has contact; (2) where the incident will occur; (3) the level of sexual arousal as well as the perpetrator's own; (4) whether force or coercion is used; (5) how long these incidents continue; and (6) whether victim or perpetrator discloses sexual contact."[31]

In the case of adult rape, social pressure and physical assault are two primary methods that rapists use to coerce sexual activity.[32] Marie Fortune and James Poling write, "In some cases of sexual assault, it is very apparent that sexuality becomes a means of expressing and discharging feelings of pent-up anger and rage. The assault is characterized by physical brutality. In the power rape, it is not the offender's desire to harm his victim, but to possess her sexually. Sexuality becomes a means of compensating for underlying feelings of inadequacy and serves to express issues of mastery, strength, control, authority, identity and capability. His goal is sexual conquest and he uses only the amount of force necessary to accomplish his objective. A third pattern is sadism in which the pain and torture of the victim creates sexual gratification."[33]

Finally, in the case of partner violence, "clinicians who work with wife batterers believe that the abusers act primarily out of an expression of the need for power and control. Feeling entitled to dominate wives or girlfriends, such men are willing to enforce their dominance with physical abuse. Highly dependent, often emotionally isolated from others, they try to control and possess their spouses. Another type of batterer physically abuses children. Sometimes he batters both wife and children, and sometimes, he batters only one or more children."[34]

These kinds of attacks were present in the narratives of the women I interviewed, and they had long-term effects. In the case of the women who were sexually violated as girls, the impact of the perpetrator's abuse of power evidenced itself in subsequent revictimization in later relationships that involved battering (Eliza and Camille); coerced sexual activity within a marriage (Rori); and emotional abuse (Tamara). In the case of Octavia (who was an adult at the time of her rape) the effects of having been sexually harassed at various points leading up to her rape, and the rape itself, resulted in her having intense concerns for her basic safety and self-worth as a human being. In all of these abuses (childhood sexual abuse, rape, and battering) power was the central organizing feature of the violent encounters. Ultimately, it was experiences of "power within" (self-determination and reliance upon a reconstructed spirituality) and relationships based on "power within community" (support and uplift experienced in encounters with OtherMothers, Sisterfriends, and Cultural selfobjects) that supported their self-recovery from abuses of power. For this reason, clinical sensitivity and awareness of how power is used and communicated should orient pastoral practitioners' approach to congregation-based ritual.

The more obvious forms of "power over" in ritual (subtle use of threats to coerce participation; threats of isolation or communal rejection if one refuses to participate; or threatening safety if someone tells outsiders about the ritual practice) are easy to notice. Other, less obvious ways in which women are at risk of being exposed to "power over" in ritual are equally important. Examples include the implied assumption that a woman's presence at the ritual indicates that she will participate and how she will participate; use of language and symbols to convey essentialist notions of identity and sexuality; gender-binding notions of women's place and value in community; and metaphors that constrict women's ability to see themselves in the image of God. While attention to these items is necessary when convening ritual space for anyone, the convergence of gender, violence, and abusive use of power that women experience in intimate violence warrants particular sensitivity.

Obtaining consent and clear communication about the intent of the ritual space and the ritual process is one of the ways to communicate "power with" and "power within" as organizing principles in WomanistCare ritual space. Leaders convening ritual space should be clear (with themselves as well as in dialogue with participants) in communicating that participation in the ritual is entirely voluntary and that the aim is to affirm them, rather than to create additional barriers to healing and community. The leaders can achieve this by clearly communicating right at the beginning what the ritual involves and continually couching appeals for participation in the language of invitation and noncoercive hospitality. While the women who come forward to participate in ritual do so of their own volition, it is the ritual conveners' responsibility to maintain emotional and spiritual safety by reinforcing that each woman may choose how she wishes to participate. Every effort should be made to optimize each participant's sense of freedom and choice so as not to replicate "power over" (directly or indirectly) and unwittingly retraumatize participants.

All of this should take place with a third clinical consideration in mind—that of posttraumatic intrapsychic splitting that can result from intimate violence. I will say more about psychotherapeutic response in the next chapter's discussion of Womanist pastoral counseling, but something should be said here in the context of conversation about ritual as a congregation-based form of pastoral care. Therapeutic engagement in any form (be it communal ritual or one-on-one counseling) takes posttraumatic stress seriously in caring for Black women. This requires practitioners to be mindful of dualistic ritual language that splits self, life events, and ethical principles into all-good or all-bad categories. Perpetuating such categories prevents persons from holding in tension the good and bad aspects of one's own self, others, and God which is necessary for healthy psychological and spiritual functioning. Taking seriously the psychological well-being of traumatized women also involves taking as much care as possible not to exacerbate traumatic transference that can and often does emerge in group settings. This is related to maintaining safe space, but it requires an additional therapeutic attunement to intragroup dynamics and the group's transference onto one another, including practitioners. Two things stand out concerning this critical piece. First, if the leaders convening the ritual space do not have a clinical background and training experience on the dynamics of trauma and intimate violence, they should be sure to include in the ritual someone who does have this experience. This additional layer of care provides support for participants (and perhaps for leaders convening the ritual space) who may directly or vicariously experience particularly painful memories during the ritual. Secondarily, it is equally important for those who facilitate ritual spaces like this to be diligent in their own self-care. I address this further in the following chapter.

WomanistCare ritual provides practitioners with a resource for orchestrating communal care in congregational settings that resonate with Black women's everyday strategies for self-recovery. While ritual provides a communal context for acknowledgment, care, and healing, it cannot be the only therapeutic option that churches make available for responding to the traumatic sequelae of intimate and cultural violence. Offering ritual space is an important first step for congregations because it draws the community's awareness to a collective pain that needs to be tended to. It also creates an opportunity for pastoral care providers who facilitate these spaces to begin conversations about deeper levels of intrapsychic healing through the support that a counseling relationship offers. Some of the women I interviewed demonstrated patterns and behaviors that suggest wounded intrapsychic structures as a result of early violence, others did not; however, patterns in their narratives invite further conversation about the psychological and relational impact of prominent intrapsychic defenses invoked to fend off the effects of traumatic experiences.

I am reminded of Foster-Boyd's caution that many avoid formal, institutionalized counseling because of the stigma attached to it, as well as the economic barriers. However, when informed by the cultural awareness that working images of WomanistCare promote, pastoral counseling that takes this awareness seriously opens up important opportunities for counseling that are sensitive to the impact of cultural countertransference. In addition, given the growing interest in partnerships between congregations and licensed professionals (pastoral counselors, marriage and family therapists, professional counselors, licensed clinical social workers) who often offer sliding-scale counseling fees, economic barriers no longer remain to receiving comprehensive care. Taken together, these two developments make the case for how counseling can become a viable option for deeper healing work with African American women who have experienced intimate and cultural violence. I take this up in the following chapter's discussion of a trauma-sensitive approach to Womanist pastoral counseling, including focus on areas of challenge and healing resources that surfaced in conversations with the women I interviewed.

5

Womanist Pastoral Counseling: Clinical Considerations

This concluding chapter considers a psychodynamic counseling response to intrapsychic struggles stemming from childhood sexual abuse, molestation, incest, rape, partner violence, and to a cultural context that normalizes these offenses. The discussion details the traumatic sequelae (aftereffects) of intimate violence and brings trauma theory into conversation with Kohutian ideas on the use of empathy to work through traumatic transference and shame. I close out the chapter with a discussion of how to engage Black women's spirituality as a resource in therapeutic conversations.

Recognizing Traumatic Sequelae

Part of the practitioners work is to be aware of the clusters of symptoms associated with trauma so that they can support women in identifying and coming to a point of clarity about violence in their lives. In *The Cry of Tamar: Violence against Women and the Church's Response*,[1] Pamela Cooper-White points out that because the trauma of childhood sexual assault happens at a point when children lack the cognitive and emotional skills to comprehend or the confidence to communicate about the abuse, it is not uncommon that adults who have experienced abuse are unaware that their posttraumatic stress disorder (PTSD) symptoms are related to sexual assault perpetrated against them when they were children. Common aftereffects in adulthood can be grouped into the following categories:

- *Fears and anxieties* (such as being alone in the dark, panic attacks, unexplainable fears)
- *Numbing and dissociative reactions* (spacing out during sex, losing sense of time, out-of-body experiences, holes in childhood memory, escapism, intrusive memories or flashbacks)
- *Physical symptoms* (gastrointestinal problems, somatization of emotional pain—headaches, gynecological disorders, pain during intercourse that may not have a physiological cause)
- *Emotional symptoms* (depression, bouts of rage or physically attacking a partner or child, unstable emotional reactions)
- *Lack of self care, self-destructive behavior and self-injury* (not feeling at home in one's body or not taking good care of one's body, manipulating body size to avoid sexual attention, eating disorders, excessive use of alcohol and/or drugs, compulsive behaviors, high risk-taking alternating with inability to take risks, self-mutilation, self injury, suicidal thoughts and attempts)
- *Difficulties in interpersonal relationships, including sexual difficulties* (inability to maintain intimate relationships, being too clingy or distant, constantly testing people, expecting to be left or taken advantage of, being hypervigilant or controlling; feeling crazy, different, dirty or unreal, a secret sense of inner badness, perfectionism, being "other directed," self hatred, inability to recognize inappropriate behavior toward oneself, intrusion, violation or danger; aversion to certain or all sexual thoughts, fantasies of abuse during sex, compulsive masturbation, frequent "impersonal" sexual contacts with many partners but inability to have sex in an intimate relationship, prostitution, other forms of sexual acting out).[2]

Taken together, these traumatic sequelae represent intrapsychic processes, personal behaviors, and interpersonal contexts that reflect the ongoing struggle of the adult survivor of childhood assault to self-regulate inner self-states and connect with others, while fearing the very connections they desire.

Unlike childhood sexual abuse, adult rape occurs long after the developmental periods of infancy and adolescence have ended and the foundation for interpersonal relations have already formed. Adults who experience sexual assault will likely display classic symptoms of PTSD (nightmares, sleep problems, startle responses and hyper vigilance, and physical symptoms like nausea and headaches)[3] and attempts to manage those symptoms. These symptoms also occur within a larger context of rape trauma syndrome. This larger context includes the following three stages that are important to recognize when supporting women who have experienced intimate violence:

- *Impact stage* (lasts several weeks to several months following the attack and includes disorganization and disruption of normal coping mechanisms, shock, fear—including fear of retaliation, anxiety, withdrawal, crying, unexpected outburst, self-blame, intrusive reliving of the events of the rape, and PTSD symptoms.)
- *Recoil or pseudo-adjustment stage* (lasting from several months to several years, the victim appears to be coping well and to have adjusted. Symptoms may diminish, although many may remain unbeknownst to others; fears may be managed, but not worked out.)
- *Integration or reorganization stage* (the assault is put into some personal sense of perspective, however the individual woman defines it, and most symptoms are gone. Still the victim may experience brief periods of depression and have occasional setbacks. Normal developmental changes and major stresses through her life can trigger assault-related emotions.)[4]

Finally, traumatic sequelae related to partner violence (battering) is similar to childhood sexual assault and adult rape in that it too causes PTSD. I use the term "partner violence" to address the wide range of behaviors in intimate relationships that are acts of violation but that do not always include extreme physical or sexual abuse. In this sense the term partner violence is used to define psychological, economic, physical, and sexual behaviors directed at maintaining power and control over a partner. Oftentimes occurring across a significant stretch of time, prolonged experience of terror causes PTSD, while also impacting interpersonal relating in ways that are similar to behaviors observed in prisoners of war. Psychiatrist Judith Herman observes that the prolonged nature of living in a context that threatens her survival has the power to order her psyche around the limited goal of survival and to significantly impact her capacity for healthy boundaries. The results of this can include:

> Diminished self esteem; being anxious to please; indecisiveness, inability to plan, inability to project into the future (violence has interrupted her life so planning seems futile), depression that is sometimes major clinical and suicidal, flattened affect to numb oneself against terror, mood swings, being jumpy, nervous, irritable, or drifting off into daydreams.[5]

PTSD and Traumatic Transference

PTSD is a real response to intimate violence, and being able to help women recognize and understand how it may be at play in their lives is an important aspect of healing. In *Trauma and Recovery: The Aftermath of Violence; from Domestic Abuse to Political Terror*,[6] Herman demystifies PTSD by examining the complex physical and psychological processes involved in the formation of memories and unconscious recall of traumatic events. At the time of the event, defensive physiological processes are set in motion to ward off the threat in the environment. These physiological changes occur primarily in the senses (vision, hearing, taste, touch, smell). As some senses shut down, others remain active, and oftentimes become overstimulated. The result is a heightened sensitivity in the senses that remained active, and lack of sensitivity in others for periods of time long after the traumatic event has actually passed. The cognitive effect is that the mind breaks up the narrative storyline of the event. Unlike regular memories, traumatic memories are stored in a way that lacks integration. People who have experienced trauma can't always recall the sequence of events, because traumatic memories are not stored sequentially. What they do have, however, is a recurring, fragmented narrative. This broken narrative is accompanied by intense repetition of physical sensations that originally occurred during the traumatic event.

This is a particularly significant point of awareness for pastoral practitioners whose therapeutic lenses are informed by psychological theory *and* theology. Here we see the usefulness of Kelly Brown Douglas's critiques of classic views of the incarnation. Her critique, in conjunction with Herman's medical insight about the biological dimensions of trauma, prompts us to closely examine any underlying theological commitment to a disembodied view of the incarnation that substantiates dualistic regard for the spirit over and against loving regard for bodies that carry the weight of trauma. It is very difficult, if not impossible, to take care for traumatized bodies seriously when one's theological commitments rest on the belief that the body (the flesh) is inherently sinful; and, thus any trauma it experiences ought to be considered part of the process of salvation through suffering. Taken together, Herman and Douglas's insights make a course correction that empowers effective response to trauma.

Herman identifies three unconscious processes (hyperarousal, intrusion, and constriction) that provide important concepts for understanding the aftereffects (sequelae) of the psychophysiological changes enacted to survive traumatic experience. Hyperarousal describes the psychophysiological changes that take place in the nervous system during an intensely threatening event. These are the physical processes in the body that are cued by cognitive and psychological awareness of threats in the environment. Hyperarousal manifests in a combination of generalized anxiety symptoms and specific fears. Concerning persons struggling with hyperarousal, Herman explains,

> They do not have a normal "baseline" level of alert but relaxed attention. Instead, they have an elevated baseline of arousal: their bodies are always on the alert for danger. They also have an extreme startle response to unexpected stimuli, as well as an intense reaction to specific stimuli associated with the traumatic event.[7]

Herman observes that over time, prolonged experience of hyperarousal has the capacity to recondition the nervous system and significantly impact physical health.

Next Herman directs attention to intrusion as the psychological process of reliving the traumatic event as if it continues to recur in the present. "They cannot resume the normal course of their lives, for the trauma repeatedly interrupts. It is as if time stops at the moment of trauma. The traumatic moment becomes

encoded in an abnormal form of memory, which breaks sponta-
neously into consciousness as flashbacks during waking states
and traumatic nightmares during sleep."[8]

Finally, constriction is the unconscious psychophysiological
attempt to alter consciousness such that the individual becomes
numb to recall of the traumatic threat. In this state events continue to register in awareness, but it is as though these events
have been disconnected from the emotional significance, and
therefore, the pain of the event:

> Perceptions may be numbed or distorted, with partial anesthesia
> or the loss of particular sensation. Time sense may be altered,
> often with a sense of slow motion, and the experience may lose
> its quality of ordinary reality. The person may feel as though the
> event is not happening to her, as though she is observing from
> outside her body, or as if the whole experience is a bad dream
> from which she will shortly awake.[9]

Each of these maneuvers involves unconsciously motivated
physiological and psychological processes that occur in concert with one another to constitute a "dialectic of trauma"[10]:
oscillation between intrusive memories of traumatic events and
constricting maneuvers to press the trauma back out of psychological and physiological awareness:

> She finds herself [or himself] caught between the extremes of
> amnesia or of reliving the trauma, between floods of intense,
> overwhelming feeling and arid states of no feeling at all, between
> irritable, impulsive action and complete inhibition of action.[11]

Addictions, risky sexual behavior, self-harming/mutilation,
and clusters of traumatic sequelae described above should
all be interpreted as efforts to manage the dialectic of terror.
Intrapsychically, the self becomes organized around defenses
initially enacted to survive the traumatic event(s). The dialectic
of bouncing between amnesia (repression) and "arid states of
no feeling at all"[12] (dissociation) significantly impacts intrapsychic functioning and interpersonal relations. Interpersonally,
relations (including the therapeutic alliance) take on an all-or-

nothing quality as the individual attempts to connect, while at the same time fearing that the connection will lead to another traumatic violation. As a result "traumatic transference"[13] underscores interpersonal relating, and its presentation in the therapeutic relationship should be regarded as the counselors' first indication of a possible trauma history.

Herman's analysis opens up a view of the processes at play in traumatic transference that are often initially misunderstood as indicative of characterological pathology:

> Some of the most astute observations on the vicissitudes of traumatic transference appear in the classic accounts of the treatment of borderline personality disorder, written when the traumatic origin of the disorder was not yet known. In these accounts, a destructive force appears to intrude repeatedly into the relationship between therapist and patient. This force, which was traditionally attributed to the patient's innate aggression, can now be recognized as the violence of the perpetrator. The psychiatrist Eric Lister remarks that the transference in traumatized patients does not reflect a simple dyadic relationship, but rather a triad: "The terror is as though the patient and therapist convene in the presence of yet another person. The third image is the victimizer, who...demanded silence and whose command is now being broken."[14]

Traumatic transference represents memories (some with fragmented narratives to hold them together and others existing as mere physical sensations) that recall experiences of terror and helplessness. This sense of helplessness is actively present when individuals engage in extremely intense merger with others (including counselors) onto whom they project the image of the ideal rescuer. Inevitably, the counselor fails to live up to this idealization and is subsequently de–idealized as incompetent, threatening, and even dangerous. In people for whom traumatic transference underscores their mode of relating, all interpersonal engagements are characterized by oscillation between extremes of self and other as "all good" or "all bad" because of posttraumatic defenses enacted to survive the inaugural threatening event. In the actual traumatic event(s), survival required dissociation and repression. However, these defenses outlive their purpose when they orient the individual's sense of all others (including those who do not pose a threat).

The result is an intense cycle of projection and reaction formation. This unconscious dynamic sabotages interpersonal efforts to connect, including the connections that undergird the therapeutic alliance. While its capacity to sabotage is clear, traumatic transference should be interpreted as unconscious efforts to (1) connect while at the same time fending off the fear of repeated violation; (2) expel painful and abusing inner objects; and (3) break the silence about what has been done to them and how they have suffered.

It is important to note that although the defenses enacted in posttraumatic splitting resemble narcissistic defenses, there is a difference between posttraumatic defenses and narcissistic pathology. The age at the time of occurrence and severity of the violence determines whether or not the event may have caused a narcissistic wound and invoked defenses around which the entire personality structure coalesced. Not all persons demonstrating narcissistic pathology have experienced intimate violence, and not all persons who have experienced intimate violence have personalities organized around narcissistic wounds. What is apparent, however, is that many women who come to therapy demonstrating traumatic transference have experienced intimate violence, and in such cases the symptoms should first be explored in light of a possible trauma history.

Like Herman, other feminist theorists and relational psychotherapeutic practitioners[15] have done much to support this diagnostic reframing. Rejecting diagnostic labels that pin traumatic transference on character defects is part of a clinical approach that takes seriously the intrapsychic consequences of trauma. Rather than locate the genesis of traumatic transference in inherently flawed intrapsychic structures (which leads to stigmatizing diagnostic categories like borderline, histrionic, and dependent), Cooper-White, Herman, Christie Neuger, and others redefine traumatic transference and maladaptive behaviors as "adaptive rather than pathological...responses to untenable double binds,"[16] those like the tenuous relationship between childhood abuse victims and their perpetrators (especially so in cases of incest); women and their abusive partners; and women and the institutions upon which they depend, but that also oppress them.

In taking this clinical stance, counselors taken a countercultural approach to diagnosis which then informs how they work with women through traumatic transference and shame.

Shame

Womanist pastoral theologian Carolyn A. L. McCrary writes of how when she listened to women who had experienced abuse, they clung to idealized notions of those who perpetrated abuse against them as if a part of themselves was at stake in letting go of this idealized image.[17] We observed this in the stories that Cirene and Eliza shared about how they idealized their abusers and subsequently developed fantasies about who they were in relation to them. A second look, however, clarified that the fantasies covered over a painful sense of shame that often sat in the background of their struggles to feel whole—as if they truly bore the imprint of God's blessing that they are good, very good. Although the force of unwanted sex and physical violence that the women experienced resulted in shame, the shame they carried was not really their own. Helping women put this shame back where it belongs is complicated because of the multiple cultural processes that keep it displaced and literally in women's laps.

Fortune points out that shame is complicated and often further compounded by religious traditions that pin the blame for women's defilement on their own embodiment and behavior.[18] The result is that women are made to carry a shame that rightfully belongs first to the people who directly abuse them, and secondarily to cultural processes and institutions that scapegoat women for others' violence towards them. This scapegoating is well observed in stereotypes and mythologies that portray Black females as Mouthy Sapphires (who deserve to be put into their place), lascivious Jezebels (who want "it" all the time), and Mammies (who couldn't possibly be raped because no one wants them anyway). Political scientist Melissa V. Harris-Perry reminds us, "These myths influence how Black women see themselves and how they understand their struggle. Most important, these myths make Black women feel ashamed."[19] While the sociohistoric analysis of Black feminists and Womanists help us to see these cultural connections, it is equally important to consider the role of Black religious institutions as mediators and/or mitigators of these narratives that normalize violence against women. Many of these cultural processes are grounded in religious beliefs that female sexuality is intrinsically sinful. Fortune points out,

> The dominant culture persists in the belief that "good" women do not get raped. Underlying this belief is the idea that if she had been behaving in a proper, righteous manner she would not have been assaulted.[20]

In these religiocultural beliefs, justification of women's abuse is ontologically rooted in their gender and sexuality. For Black women it is rooted in their gender, sexuality, *and* race. These religious beliefs are present in multiple cultural rules about who is deemed acceptable and who is not, because of underlying (often unacknowledged) assumptions about the sinfulness of women's bodies. In spite of the fact that these rules misdirect shame at women who are violated rather than at the people who abuse them and are grounded in racialized religious myths, these social rules are still very powerful in the spiritual beliefs that Black females encounter.

The power of these rules is well observed in the shame that many harbor over intimate violence that forces them to carry their abuser's shame, which is then compounded by messages in culture that misinterprets their violation as evidence of their failure to uphold important religiocultural standards. The result is a compounded sense of shame.

McCrary defines shame as "an overall self-attribution of failure and 'wrongness.' It is a global self-interpretation that *I* am wrong. *I* failed. Even, *I* am worthless."[21] Referencing Michael Lewis, McCrary clarifies this kind of shame as

> a total self-failure vis-à-vis standards, rules or goals. Shame is the product of a complex set of cognitive activities in the evaluation of an individual's action in regard to standards, rules, goals and global self.[22]

This shame is the global, overwhelming sense that who she is—not what she has done (as is the case in feelings of guilt)—is bad and wrong, and it occurs when there is failure to meet an important rule or standard. The shame that Black females incur is due in part to having failed to uphold arbitrary gender rules that would have protected them against violence had they somehow just *been* different.

The compounded nature of this shame invokes multiple conscious and unconscious defensive responses in Black women. Some of these function to protect them against an inner sense of badness, while they also create a barrier against further cultural violence. Drawing on Donald Nathanson, Cooper-White identifies four defensive responses to shame: (1) withdrawal (running away from the offending stimulus; becoming silent); (2) attacking oneself ("Yes, officer, of course I'll be more careful—thank you for the advice"); (3) avoidance (turning to alcohol, drugs, or distracting the other with a source of pride—"Look at my new car! See something else besides what I can't stand to see about myself"); or (4) attacking the other (attempting to reduce shame by reducing the self-worth of the other—physical or sexual abuse, contempt, character assassination, banter, and put-downs).[23]

These shame responses are enacted to fend off psychic disintegration and interior feelings of shame. In the context of intimate and cultural violence, these defenses protect pain, vulnerability, and a desecrated sense of exposure that lie at the center of shame. They also provide methods that allow women to manage the shaming effects of a victim-blaming culture wherein female bodies are the cause of gender-based violence. For Black women, race adds an additional layer to the cultural message that their own bodies (Black, female, and, for some, same-gender loving) are to blame for the violence they experience.

When Black women enact these unconscious defenses, in addition to covering over the fact of intimate violence, the defensive functions also provide them the means to create a mask that protects them from cultural assaults and religiocultural beliefs about Black female sexuality and morality. Being able to withdraw and/or become silent about violence, using self-effacing comments to hide one's true feelings (attacking oneself), avoidance that distracts others from seeing their hurt, and even attacking others: all this protects them by deflecting attention away from their real experience of vulnerability and defilement. bell hooks uses the term, "practice of dissimulation,"[24] to describe the methods Black women employ to fend off shame and racial violence. Darlene Clark-Hine describes this maneuvering as a "culture of dissemblance"[25] in which Black women maintain a public facade to obscure and protect their pain from others who may or may not display compassion towards them. To be clear, within the context of intimate violence, shame defenses are first concerned with concealing the pain and sense of wrongness that comes with embodying the effects of someone else's violating act. However, it is equally important to acknowledge the role that shame defenses play in providing Black women with a barrier between themselves and additional layers of cultural shame. For these women, shame is highly complex.

The compounded shame from intimate and cultural violence not only impacts Black women physically and intrapsychically, but it also has a spiritual dimension. Shame defenses create barriers between self and other, but the feelings of devalued self-worth in the eyes of one's abuser and culture also inculcate a sense of distance and diminished value in God's eyes. The sense of unacceptability in the eyes of God and others is a spiritual consequence of defiling intimate and cultural assaults, and it is a primary condition from which Black women who have experienced violence need to heal and recover.

Empathic Work with Trauma and Shame

As a reminder, many women enter therapy for support in dealing with any number of traumatic sequelae described above without much conscious awareness of the connections between their counseling concerns and traumatic experience in their history. As counselees establish transference with the therapist, the traumatic nature of the transference brings the presence of the abuser and abusive context into the therapeutic relationship. Again, at this point the counselee may or may not be aware of the traumatic source of their transference, and counselors should be careful to allow the narrative to unfold without pressure to detail or confess the traumatic experience. Doing so only replicates her abuser's use of "power over" and undermines therapy. Instead, work should be done to gain the counselee's trust by careful listening not only for the narrative, but more importantly, for the emotional content of experience as it unfolds over time.

This process is filled with (and can become characterized by) enactments of the trauma narrative that frustrate both the counselee and counselor as they struggle together through unarticulated (unspeakable) memories of terror and helplessness. For the counselee the unconscious motivation behind this traumatic transference is to determine whether or not her counselor will damage her (emotionally, physically, or even sexually by violating the boundaries of the helping relationship) like others have in the past. Response in the counselor's countertransference must be constantly monitored for the clues they provide about the nature of the trauma, the counselee's interior experience, and the counselor's own reaction formations. This is the nature of the working-through process that heals intrapsychic wounds by providing empathically attuned responses that differ qualitatively from the empathically failing response embedded in abusive and painful encounters.

Self Psychological theory's response to this kind of traumatic transference consists of well-timed empathic responses (Kohut's two-step move from acknowledgment to interpretation) that build up the ability to integrate the good and bad experiences of self and others by gradually working through traumatic transference. By focusing on cultivating an empathically resonant self-object experience, practitioners help clients build up the interior capacity to be in touch with their own ability to regulate affect and maintain a sense of themselves as separate, yet still related to others. These are normal developmental tasks for everyone. For women who were sexually and physically abused as children, or adult women who have had extensive experiences of torture in battering relationships, this development has been interrupted. The prolonged nature may be further complicated by the absence of either a language or narrative to describe what they may recall physiologically, but which they cannot describe verbally because of repression or because the violation happened during a stage of their development that predates the language and cognitive capacity for articulation.

Kohut emphasized empathy as an affective, intuitive, and intellectual process in which counselors put "yourself into the shoes of, think yourself appropriately into the inner life of another person."[26] In an article titled "On Empathy," he described a two-step process that is helpful in this work. The first step involved conveying that the client had indeed been felt, which is then followed by a secondary interpretation of the unempathic frustrations which have led to the intense vulnerabilities. This empathy is a core component in care that addresses self–structures wounded by unempathic nurturing environments. It is also helpful in addressing post-traumatic splitting that is not narcissistic in its genesis, but which nevertheless presents similarly:

> I believe that the move from understanding to explaining, from confirming that the analyst knows what the patient feels and thinks and imagines (that he's in tune with his inner life), and the next step of giving of interpretations is a move from a lower form of empathy to a higher form of empathy. Interpretations are not intellectual constructions. If they are, they won't work; [they might work] accidentally, but not in principle. A good analyst reconstructs the childhood past in the dynamics of the current transference with warmth, with understanding for the intensity of the feelings, and with the fine understanding of the various secondary conflicts that intervene as far as the expression of these [childhood wishes and needs] are concerned.[27]

An important aspect of Kohut's formulation concerns his overall awareness that while empathy is the main element that stimulates growth in the developing intrapsychic structure of a child, empathy continues to facilitate intrapsychic growth across the life span. The need for empathy doesn't stop in adolescence; it is a basic human need that persists throughout one's development and life. The "good" analyst that Kohut describes makes available his/her own healthy, mature self as the focus for the client's traumatic transference and search for empathic resonance. As a merger experience ensues, inevitably a misstep on the part of the therapist will rupture the empathic connection, and it is in redressing the misstep that the opportunity for growth presents itself. As counselee and counselor work through empathic ruptures, empathically failing selfobject experiences are displaced by other empathically resonant experiences that strengthen the self-structure. In counseling with women who have experienced intimate and cultural violence, empathy, then, is the process whereby traumatic transference is addressed by counselors' attunement and careful response to traumatic experiences of terror and helplessness.

The building up of empathically resonant experience through transmuting internalization breaks down amnestic walls separating split-off persecutory and painful inner objects that are split off into "all good" or "all bad" representations. What begins to emerge is a self-empathy that creates a capacity to tolerate conscious awareness that both "good" and "bad" actually exist together in the person(s) and institutions that persecutory and painful inner objects represent. In this process of integration, giving up the idealized ("all good") images of traumatic inner objects allows the woman to acknowledge previously repressed shameful experiences and disavowed representations of the self in relation to the abuser. This is an especially significant moment for women whose experience with intimate violence began in childhood and whose survival required dependence upon adults who were also their abusers, as well as other adults (the nonoffending primary care provider) who may have been directly or indirectly complicit in the abuse.

Recall Eliza's experience of incest. It was years after the abuse ended when Eliza realized that the father she adoringly remembered was also a great source of her pain ("my beloved father had treated me like I was his wife, his woman, his bitch, his whore"). This moment was significant for her because it allowed her to identify the source of her pain and to connect abuse to the coping strategies she developed to manage this pain.

For Camille, her father's confession that he had protected her abuser broke the family's denial and her commitment to the role she played as the nice girl who didn't cause much trouble. As the image of her relationship with the family fell apart, she could acknowledge the source of her pain and the anger she felt toward her family for prioritizing her uncle's freedom over the justice she deserved as a child who had been traumatized by rape. Being able to deal openly with this shame also had spiritual consequences. This anger and hunger for justice was part of her struggle to forgive. Camille was unwilling to focus her attention on forgiveness until she experienced justice in her family. In both situations Eliza and Camille gave up idealized images of their abusers, the abusive contexts, and themselves, which allowed them to access and work on selfrecovery. For Camille, this also included her ambivalence concerning forgiveness.

The ambivalent nature of her feelings about forgiveness resonated with Marie M. Fortune's observation of how society and families often place the burden of forgiveness and unreasonable expectations on the shoulders of those who have been violated:

> In situations of violence or abuse, forgiveness is the last step, at best. But, it can hold a key to healing. In Christian circles, forgiveness is the single most common expectation that is placed on victims of clergy abuse, rape, incest, battering, etc. Many people say to victims and survivors: "The Bible says you must forgive and forget"; Never mind that it is impossible to forget the things the abuser did; never mind that "forgive and forget" appears in Shakespeare's *King Lear* (IV:vii), not the Bible. Never mind that it is the worst advice we can give any survivor. She takes it seriously and tries very hard "to forgive," absent any acknowledgement on the abuser's part of the harm he has done, not to mention any effort on his part to change.[28]

Forgiveness is a slow process that should occur with the interests of the person who experienced the trespass leading any possible steps. The emphasis should be placed on these needs, rather than the abuser and the community's need for the woman to hurry along. Hurrying along runs two risks: first, it suggests an inauthentic gesture that denies that pain is still unresolved; second, it pre-empts any real possibility for forgiveness that comes when a woman is able to confront God, self, and community over the traumatic violation. Fortune reminds us that if/when forgiveness happens, it is a gift for the survivor (not the abuser) that comes out of her hard won transformation of the meaning she has made of the traumatic experience.

These important (yet painful) selfobjects include cultural selfobjects—symbols, language, and popular figures that reflect distorted images of Black womanhood. For Rori, the Black church she grew up in was one of these cultural selfobjects. In addition to being the space where she regularly encountered the clergy person who abused her, the Black church was also a context for cultural assaults against Black women. She felt that the religious and gender socialization she received in church set her up to become a woman who followed strict guidelines that she felt played a role in the battering she experienced at the hands of the man she married. When the abuse became too much, she left the relationship and began questioning what she had been taught. The abuse provided her an opportunity to de-idealize the church and to see its theology for what it was: a mediator of cultural assumptions that contributes to and normalizes intimate violence. While she mourned this loss, the mourning itself allowed her to reconsider in what kind of church and theology she would like to call her own.[29]

In Cirene's exploration of Buddhism and African Traditional Religions, we can observe another example of how, in working through shame and forgiveness, some Black women may need to mourn the loss of the Black church. In the interviews she talked about the non-judgmental environment she experienced in the Buddhist temple. While her appreciation of Buddhism may suggest that she idealized this religious context, even this idealization offers insight into the loss she experienced in the sexist, homophobic theology and culture she encountered in the Black church. Inasmuch as she also found mentors there, the loss of the Black church as a cultural selfobject that affirmed her was still real. Cultural selfobjects must also be mourned for the loss they represent in failing to provide empathic contexts for Black women's intimate and cultural pain. Referencing Martha Fowlkes, Sheppard writes,

> Fowlkes makes the case that loss resides in the social and intra-psychic spheres, and mourning leads to a transformed view of the

world and self. Fowlkes, not a practical theologian, offers a theological statement: this transformation radically alters one's tie to that which has been lost, and furthermore, this shift in attachment allows for the re-engagement with life that is creative. This transformation, then comes about through engagement with a broader, caring community, and this honest engagement is the path to hope. This we witness in Lamentations, hope begins to emerge in the naming of the suffering and in the midst of mourning.[30]

This experience of loss and grief is at once both pivotal and painful. On the one hand, women may find relief in identifying the source of their struggles in someone's abuse of them, as opposed to believing they alone are to blame. On the other hand, this new revelation can be particularly painful because formerly disavowed and threatening emotions surface. One of these emotions is the shame that emerges when women are able to give up (mourn) idealized images of themselves in relation with abusive selfobjects and cultural selfobjects. The vulnerability that comes with exposing the source of a woman's shame can be overwhelming. Response to this shame should not be to fix it, but rather to walk with the counselee through it, all the while listening for clues about the role that this shame plays in her overall self-concept. For some, it is rooted in a sense that they were to blame for the violence they experienced. For example, Octavia initially blamed herself for being gang raped. This self-blame was part of a larger vulnerability concerning her spiritual struggles to connect with God. She interpreted the violence as God's judgment against her for not having properly connected with God. She became able to let go of the shame and self-blame when she developed a distinctly female view of God inside of herself. Pushing her to give up this shame prematurely would have usurped her efforts to find the source of it.

Counseling provides a therapeutic alliance that is willing and capable of providing a container for these extremely intense feelings, unspeakable memories of defiling abuse, and its attendant traumatic transference. This same therapeutic container also provides the context for supporting Black women in dealing with the personal behaviors and interpersonal relationships that occur alongside the intrapsychic dynamics in traumatic sequelae.

This involves supporting women in first making connections between how they feel and the trauma they've experienced through processes I described above. It also involves listening and supporting women in building awareness of how the trauma is also related to the personal behaviors and adaptive coping strategies they used (drug and alcohol abuse, hypersexuality, self-mutilation, risky and dangerous behaviors, dissociative sexual encounters) to manage the memories and psychophysiological symptoms of childhood sexual abuse, adult rape, and partner violence.

Therapeutic work in this area looks like conversations about organizing networks of care that help women resume their day-to-day activities by walking them to and from their cars and calling to check-in. It looks like developing safety plans with women who are currently experiencing partner violence; safety contracts with women who demonstrate proclivity to harm themselves or others; and ongoing efforts to cultivate self-empathy that supports women and strengthens their capacity to establish and hold healthy boundaries that protect them against further violation. In particular, the safety contract provides a baseline for safety by establishing clear parameters detailing the counselee and counselor's commitment for how they will agree to respond if and/or when physical or psychological safety is at risk of being compromised.

Finally, the therapeutic container must also be capable of creating opportunities to acknowledge and engage Black women's faith as a resource that can be integrated into the healing work done in one-on-one counseling.

Spirituality as Therapeutic Resource

The women's responses in interviews pointed to spirituality as a connection with God that provided the context for wrestling ultimate meaning out of daily experience. This translated into their belief that God had an ultimate plan and fulfilling purpose for their lives in spite of experiences that defiled them. Paying attention to these experiences, and not just for the purposes of deconstructing them as split-off idealizations of themselves in relationship with God, creates an opportunity for practitioners to learn about Black women's everyday ways of confronting and challenging violence—which is a critical aspect of healing.

Rori, Tamara, and Cirene each talked about particular encounters in which the mystical nature of the experience let them know that God was actively extending a connection and communicating specifically with them about the circumstances of their lives—even their pain. For Rori these spiritual experiences often revolved around her ancestors and living members of the family who were transitioning into ancestorship.

Rori recognized that the relationships she had with her ancestors were part of her relationship with God. She felt as if there were times when God sent those ancestors to connect with her at just the right time to empower her in the face of personal challenges. She explained that the visitations took away many of her fears, including fear of her own finitude.

> (Rori) For me, it took away the fear.
> (Stephanie) What took away the fear?
> (Rori) Seeing and hearing and knowing....It took away the fear of death. It took away the fear of death. Of seeing and knowing and hearing and realizing that God is eternal, that there is no end. We're thinking that, like, when we go to somebody's funeral, that that's the end. "Oh, they had such a wonderful life." But, it's not the end. That's the end of that body. So, it takes away that fear. Think about it. If you weren't afraid, what would you do? What could you do? What wouldn't you do?

A core aspect of these visits is that the visitations continued to come in the middle of her struggles, which she interpreted as God offering a familiar, sustaining protective presence even in the middle of pain like what she experienced in intimate violence. These visits were an essential phenomenon in her spirituality. She talked about how a visit in her dreams from her deceased father gave her what she needed to make up her mind about leaving an abusive relationship:

> ...And he went to the hospital and told us, he said, "It won't be long." So I saw him that Tuesday, I think it was a Tuesday and he said, "Baby, I'm not going to make it through the night." And I said, "Oh daddy, don't say that." And then, that's when I was awakened with him...His spirit told me he was gone. And I'm like daddy, don't leave us. We ain't finished harassing you [Rori smiles]....Every now and then he would call, "Baby." And I look around and...What, daddy? Or I see him in a dream and he's trying to tell me something and I be all day trying to figure out, what was he trying to tell me? And then something that would show up where I sit and it is involving [name of husband omitted] and I be like...He was trying to warn me. Okay, I gotcha. I understand.

Visits from the ancestors sustained her spirit while she worked through intimate decisions concerning her family and men in her life. Regardless of where she found herself, her relationship with the ancestors was a grounding element in her awareness of God's ongoing presence in her life.

While each of the women spoke of various experiences that made them aware of God's presence in their lives, not all of them experienced comfort in these encounters. At times these encounters were frightening because they made them acutely aware of there being a purpose for their lives, an idea they cherished but also at times feared because they didn't want to disappoint God by not living up to that purpose. Though the visions and dreams let them know God was actively engaged in their lives and concerned for them, the experiences were at times overwhelming. Tamara shared about one of these experiences that occurred during a critical moment of spiritual growth and development in her life.

> The dream started—well, the experience started off....I was in my waterbed, and there was a fog over the bed. Like I'm laying here, and there's this fog over me, and it's about this much

space [motioning with her hands] between me and the cloud. I was rolling from side to side because there were claws reaching through the cloud. I could feel them. They couldn't.... They were trying to grab me, but they couldn't. I kept rolling. It was like their hands—their claws were just kind of grabbing me. They weren't scratching me, but they couldn't *grab* me either. I kept rolling and rolling. A scripture was just pouring out of my mouth. And, then that went away. And there was this hand. Well, there was a lightning bolt, actually. No. Hold on. I'm getting ahead of myself. There was this sign. I saw this sign. So the cloud disappears, and there's this sign, and it's spelling out words. I'm... "P-o-w-e-r," and then I said, "Power." As soon as I said that, there was like a lightning bolt from heaven that— and it struck my heart. But, at the end of the lightning bolt there was a hand, and it grabbed my heart, and it started to pull like it was pulling my heart out of my chest. It was pulling, and it hurt. It was pulling, and it was pulling, and I was raising up off the bed, and it got to the point where either the hand had to let go, or it was literally going to pull my heart out of my chest. When I woke up, I was just arched up like this. For me, this sounds so crazy to me when I'm saying it, but it's like it comforts me to know that I actually have the power to make a change. I'm not doing.... I'm running from it. But, the reality of it is, is if I'm standing on the ground, I'm more afraid of success than I am of failure. I really don't fear being a failure, because I know that there is this power, this call, this something that I'm supposed to do. I'm just afraid of how far God will take me on that journey.

In Tamara's dream she felt a direct connection with God that involved her use of scripture to resist spiritual forces that she felt would harm her and the use of her voice to claim the inner power that she felt God have given her. Her awareness of this power from God maintained Tamara's belief that God had a purpose for her life. However, claiming this power and its manifestation in the gift of prophecy frightened her. In addition to various dreams, Tamara also spoke of a prophetic gift in which she heard and spoke judgment as God's intermediary about the spiritual consequences of wrongdoing she observed. This gift created a sense of ambivalence for her because, although it let her know that God was intimately involved in her life and its purpose, the fear of being judged and condemned for the spiritual consequences of things she has done in her past was a recurring obstacle to her embracing the spiritual gifts that affirm God's presence in her life. Yet, prophetic dreams and the knowledge that she possessed a sacred gift maintained her awareness of God's presence in her life. The work for women like Tamara would be to help them learn to accept the parts of themselves as whole women, not good women, or bad women, but women whom God knows and loves.

Above average skills in practical areas that put these women in a position to help transform the lives of others was for them another mark of God's active involvement in their lives. While the women were proud of their abilities, they ultimately gave God the credit for the positive impact those abilities had on the lives of others. A significant aspect of this experience involved the skills and strategies they used to survive and resist violation, and to impact the lives of others.

In this vein, Eliza's discussion of her writing ability focused on how it helped her cope with the intimate violence and subsequent feelings she faced. She also believed that her writing ability and capacity to speak publicly about abuse and violence was a gift from God that transformed the lives of others who similarly struggled. Her writing ability and willingness to be open testified to God's presence in her life in spite of defiling experiences. She spoke of these gifts and God's presence in her life as divine grace:

> I write about it because that kind of helps me to get it out, and I talk about it. I talk about it everywhere....So—what I found is that so often it helps other women then to be open. Oh, then they can feel free. [They think] "Oh, well, you [did that or had that happen]?" "Well, mine wasn't that bad." They don't say that but I think, you know, it's part of it because all of us have something and we have various degrees of dealing—and ways of dealing that we....Hearing someone else's, you know, we're able to say, "Oh, yeah, I'm still here in God's grace, God's grace." You know?

And so I'm thankful for the grace God has given me and the words that God has given me, because I flunked English. I did. But I read all the time, so I knew how it should sound. It might not have been grammatically correct, you know, but I knew how it should sound. So even in the flunking...I mean, I really flunked, okay. Sure enough, okay? Couldn't even take French because I didn't have the good grammar background. Flunked French, lil red F's going across the report card. So—but I'm a writer and I just tell people...So, you know, God can do things that we don't even think about, you know?

So maybe that's what I'm supposed to share with y'all tonight. I don't know, because I could talk about books if I could just remember them, because I read all the time so I've read all kinds of things, you know, when they come out, Pearl Cleage, you know, I read them immediately. I love her. And so, you know, I could go on, but I won't tonight. But, I did bring some of my writings.

Eliza has written several volumes of poetry, various articles, and she has been speaking publicly about healing for over twenty years. She described her work as focused on setting people "free" by using her own story as an example of how God continued to extend grace and relationship in spite of defiling experiences and shame. The impact of this grace was that she no longer hid the parts of her life that at one point caused her shame, including her positive HIV status. Instead, she shared her story because she believed her openness revealed something about God to others. For Eliza, as well as others of the women, God's transformation of everyday abilities was evidence of a divine purpose in their lives.

The narratives above demonstrate multiple ways that the women's faith provided a lens through which they could reposition the experience of violence as a part, but not the whole, of their identities. This faith also maintained a sense of connection with God that transcended the barriers of shame and defilement. They were fully aware of all they had been through, but they were able to face the memories of these traumatic experiences with the knowledge that God was deeply invested and interested in their lives. A theme running throughout these narratives concerns the communal. Be it Rori's visits from ancestors, Tamara's gift of prophetic voice concerning the spiritual well-being of others, or the prolific nature of Eliza's writing abilities, each of these experiences involved God's presence in and through community to raise awareness of God's sacred will for their lives. This was a presence that mattered because it raised their spiritual consciousness of God's sustaining presence in the middle of painful situations and God's transformation in their lives as well as in the lives of others who have similarly suffered intimate and cultural assaults.

To be clear, neither women nor the practitioners working with them can afford to set aside clinical sensitivity in hearing these stories of faith. I do not underestimate the power of intimate and cultural violence to significantly impact how Black women experience and talk about God. These narratives are indeed filled with threads of idealization and intense notes of deep despair. But, when we listen closely to the idealizations we can discern kernels that accurately speak to the way that God has moved in these women's lives, and how they have actively responded to this movement in ways that enable them to survive, sustain, and thrive.

When counselors listen for and engage these everyday strategies, they provide an opportunity for Black women to affirm their own sacred capacity to co-create with God and others the necessary opportunities to make themselves whole in spite of defiling experiences.

Conclusion

...she stood up then and danced with her twisted hip the rest of what her heart had to say, while the others opened their mouths and gave her the music.[1]

Having admonished her community to love themselves, Baby Suggs, holy stands up and dances because she knows that what she has told the community is equally valid for her. She too must practice what helps her love her inside parts. Baby, Suggs, holy offers much in the way of notes on self-care for practitioners who convene a safe space with (and for) Black women.

Self-Care

The journey with the women who trusted me to hold and handle their sacred stories was immeasurably valuable, both personally and professionally. Prioritizing and privileging their subjectivity required that I listen to them first for what they could show me about the ins, outs, and shortcomings of Psychological theory and Womanist thought. Their live stories also required that I step outside of the safe objectivity of being a detached scholar and into the intersubjective space of being impacted as I poured over their stories in search of clues on how pastoral theology can learn to recognize relevant help and its aspects. Inevitably the process raised difficult and painful memories while requiring that I grapple intellectually and personally with what their stories touched in me.

Pastoral practitioners are active participants in the journey to self-recovery, but the quality of their presence is dependent upon their own practices self-care for wounds that are their own as well as those that they develop while witnessing the pain of others. Convening Womanist space for women who have experienced intimate violence is important work that taxes the mind, body, and spirit. Witnessing the emotional recall of traumatic experience brings them face-to-face with suffering and it is common for care providers to become overwhelmed by what they hear. Carolyn Yoder names this difficult process as secondary trauma:

> Secondary or vicarious trauma refers to the effects experienced by rescue workers, caregivers, and others who respond to catastrophes and attend to direct victims firsthand. Many journalists who covered victims' testimonies in South Africa's Truth and Reconciliation Commission reported post-traumatic stress reactions, even though they were briefed beforehand on how to avoid becoming personally traumatized. The effects of secondary trauma are similar to those experienced by victims and survivors themselves.[2]

It is imperative that practitioners make their own needs for communal ritual, one-on-one counseling and professional supervision part of their ongoing preparation for facilitating safe space for others. A significant risk in this work concerns the faith crisis that commonly emerges in response to hearing atrocities that question God's presence, and even God's existence. In addition to participation in therapeutic contexts like the ones outlined in this chapter and the one before it, self-care also looks like the practitioner's commitment to communities of accountability that will call them to laugh, cry, dance, and love themselves (and the God within) fiercely. It requires carving out a safe space where others play the music for the dance of joy, or the dirge of lament that needs to take place in order that practitioners can be made whole from experiences that may indeed twist their hips, but that are yet unable to stop the will to dance.

More Work to Do

When I started the research for *A Womanist Pastoral Theology against Intimate and Cultural Violence*, my focus was Black women who have experienced intimate and cultural violence and who have significant ties with the church. Further study not limited by the initial parameters I set needs to be done to build on the insights offered in this book. For instance, pastoral theology needs to hear from younger women, under the age of eighteen, to hear their firsthand narratives of survival, interrogation, and overcoming. Additionally, African American males surviving intimate and cultural violence represent another group about whom we must learn more. Grappling theologically with one half of the community while the other remains silenced and wounded does nothing to alleviate intimate violence as a problem in and of itself—regardless of the victim's gender. We also need to hear from people (both males and females) who experienced violence at the hands of others who shared their same gender, as well as those who experienced violence at the hands of women—a particularly under-recognized group of persons who commit physical and sexual violence. More also needs to be heard from samples of women, men, and adolescents across a wider economic spectrum than what is represented in this text. While the call for participants was extended across the community, the women in this research were primarily middle class, and pastoral theology would definitely benefit from a sampling that has more diversity in terms of education and access to economic resources

Finally, there is more to be done to address the challenge that religious pluralism presents for churches, many of which have members whose Christian identity is a hybrid blend of multiple religious traditions. In order to support members in moving closer to God in the face of seemingly insurmountable pains, we must be willing to engage the many ways in which they come to a God who is often called by many names.

Notes

Introduction

1. National Center for Injury Prevention and Control, Centers for Disease Control and Prevention, *The National Intimate Partner and Sexual Violence Survey (NISVS): 2010 Summary Report* (2011), by Michele C. Black, Kathleen C. Basile, Matthew J. Breiding, Sharon G. Smith, Mikel L. Walters, Melissa T. Merrick, Jieru Chen and Mark R. Stevens. http://www.cdc.gov/violenceprevention/pdf/nisvs_report2010-a.pdf, accessed January 20, 2014.
2. Ibid., table 2.1, 18.
3. Ibid., figure 2.2, 25.
4. Ibid., figure 4.5, 49.
5. Womanist works on violence committed against Black women include: Toinette M. Eugene, "Swing Low Sweet Chariot: A Womanist Ethical Response to Sexual Violence and Abuse," in *Violence against Women and Children: A Theological Sourcebook*, ed. Marie M. Fortune and Carol J. Adams (New York: Continuum, 1995), 185–200; and Eugene, "Lifting as We Climb, Womanist Theorizing about Religion and the Family," in *Religion, Feminism and the Family*, ed. Anne E. Carr and Mary Stewart Van Leeuwen (New York: Westminster/John Knox, 1996), 330–342; Toinette Eugene and James N. Poling, *Balm for Gilead: Pastoral Care for African American Families Experiencing Abuse* (Nashville, TN: Abingdon, 1998); Cheryl Townsend Gilkes, "The 'Loves' and the 'Troubles' of African American Women's Bodies: The Womanist Challenge to Cultural Humiliation and Community Ambivalence," in *A Troubling in My Soul: Womanist Perspectives on Evil and Suffering*, ed. Emilie M. Townes (Maryknoll, NY: Orbis Books, 1993), 232–249; Linda M. Hollies, "When the Mountain Won't Move," in *Violence against Women: A Theological Sourcebook*, ed. Marie M. Fortune and Carol J. Adams (New York: Continuum, 1995), 314–327; Teresa A. Snorton, "The Legacy of the African American Matriarch: New Perspectives for Pastoral Care," in *Through the Eyes*

of Women: Insights for Pastoral Care, ed. Jeanne Stevenson Moessner (Minneapolis: Fortress Press, 1996), 50–65; Carolyn A. McCrary, "The Wholeness of Women," *Journal of the Interdenominational Theological Center,* no. 25 (June 1998): 258–294; and McCrary, "Intimate Violence against Black Women," *Journal of the Interdenominational Theological Center,* no. 28 (Fall 1998): 3–37; Traci C. West, *Wounds of the Spirit: Black Women, Violence and Resistance Ethics* (New York: New York University Press, 1999); Teresa L. Fry Brown, *God Don't Like Ugly: African American Women Handing on Spiritual Values* (Nashville, TN: Abingdon Press, 2000); Kelly Brown Douglas, *Sexuality and the Black Church: A Womanist Perspective* (Maryknoll, NY: Orbis Books, 2003); Delores S. Williams, *Sisters in the Wilderness: The Challenge of Womanist God-Talk* (Maryknoll, NY: Orbis Books, 2004); Monica A. Coleman, *The Dinah Project: A Handbook for Congregational Response to Sexual Violence* (Cleveland, OH: Pilgrim Press, 2004); Emilie N. Townes, *Womanist Ethics and the Cultural Production of Evil* (New York: Palgrave Macmillan, 2006); Chanequa Walker-Barnes, "The Burden of the Strong Black Woman," *Journal of Pastoral Theology* 19, no. 1 (Summer 2009): 1–21; Phillis I. Sheppard, "No Rose-Colored Glasses: Womanist Practical Theology and Response to Sexual Violence," In *In Spirit and in Truth: Essays on Theology, Spirituality and Embodiment in Honor of C. John Weborg,* ed. Phillip J. Anderson and Michelle Clifton Soderstrom (Chicago: Covenant Press, 2006), 241–256; and Sheppard, *Self, Culture and Others in Womanist Practical Theology* (New York: Palgrave Macmillan, 2011).

For further analysis of the cultural, religious, theological, and psychological dimensions of intimate violence read: Marie M. Fortune, *Sexual Violence: The Unmentionable Sin* (Toledo, OH: The Pilgrim Press: 1983), and Fortune, *Sexual Violence: The Sin Revisited* (Cleveland, OH: The Pilgrim Press, 2005); Rita Nakashima Brock, *Theologies by Heart: A Christology of Erotic Power* (New York: The Crossroad Publishing Company, 1988); Larry Kent Graham, *Care of Persons, Care of Worlds: A Psychosystems Approach* (Nashville, TN: Abingdon, 1992); James N. Poling, *The Abuse of Power: A Theological Problem* (Nashville, TN: Abingdon, 1991); Maxine Glaz and Jeanne Stevenson Moessner, eds., *Women in Travail and Transition: A New Pastoral Care* (Minneapolis: Augsburg, 1996); Marie M. Fortune and Carol J. Adams, eds., *Violence against Women and Children: A Theological Sourcebook* (New York: Continuum, 1995); Jeanne Stevenson Moessner, ed., *Through the Eyes of Women: Insights for Pastoral Care* (Minneapolis, MN: Fortress Press, 1996); Elaine Graham, "Practical Theology as Transforming Practice," in *Blackwell Reader in Pastoral and Practical Theology,* ed. James Woodward and Stephen Pattison (Malden, MA: Blackwell Publishing, 2000); Bonnie J. Miller-McLemore, "How Sexuality and Relationships

Have Revolutionized Pastoral Theology," in *The Blackwell Reader in Practical and Pastoral Theology*, ed. James Woodard and Stephen Pattison (Massachusetts: Blackwell Publishing, 2000), 233–247. Christie Cozad Neuger, *Counseling Women: A Narrative Pastoral Approach* (Minneapolis, MN: Fortress Press, 2001); Jeanne Stevenson Moessner and Teresa Snorton, eds., *Women out of Order: Risking Change and Creating Care in a Multicultural World* (Minneapolis, MN: Fortress Press, 2010); Pamela Cooper-White, *The Cry of Tamar: Violence against Women and the Church's Response*, 2nd edition (Minneapolis, MN: Augsburg, 2012).

6. Nancy Boyd-Franklin, *Black Families in Therapy: Understanding the African American Experience, 2nd edition.* (New York: Guilford Press, 2003), 84.

7. I borrow the term *intimate violence* from ethicist Traci C. West to encompass the multiple forms of sexual, physical, and emotional violence that women have experienced in encounters and relationships with males. These experiences include childhood sexual assault, molestation and incest, rape, and partner battering, and it also includes experiences with strangers (rape or other assault by a stranger, sexual harassment by a stranger). The use of the word "intimate" refers to the nature of the violence committed against the woman's body rather than the quality of the relationship with the perpetrator. In *Wounds of the Spirit*, West explains, "Therefore, stranger rape would still be considered intimate violence even though the assault did not take place in the context of an ongoing intimate relationship. For sexual violation of a woman's body constitutes intimate violence regardless of whether the assault occurs within a chosen relationship of intimacy or not," 104.

8. Read Patricia Hill Collins, "The Past Is Ever Present, Recognizing the New Racism," in *Black Sexual Politics: African Americans, Gender and the New Racism* (New York: Routledge, 2005), chapter 2, 53–86.

9. Townes, *Womanist Ethics*, 31.

10. Ibid., 62.

11. Ibid., 116.

12. Evelyn Brooks Higginbotham, *Righteous Discontent: The Women's Movement in the Black Baptist Church, 1880–1920* (Boston: Harvard University Press, 1994), 186–187.

13. Darlene Clark-Hine, "Rape and the Inner Lives of Black Women in the Midwest," *Signs* 14, no. 4 (Summer 1998): 915.

14. Chanequa Walker-Barnes, "The Burden of the Strong Black Woman," 4. Borrowing from Black Feminist Trudier Harris's examination of the Strong Black Woman icon (a derivative of the mammy mythology) as an example of African American strategies that counter white racist assault on Black female identity, Walker-Barnes writes, "African American authors' reinscription of the centrality of strength to Black womanhood emerges from their attempt to defy negative racial

stereotypes and to portray Black women's character as above reproach. Thus, the legacy of the SBW serves important financial, psychological, and cultural functions for African Americans, even as the suffering of Black women goes unnoticed or, worst, glorified when noticed." Read also Teresa A. Snorton's "The Legacy of the African American Matriarch," 50–65.

15. Heinz Kohut, "The Disorders of the Self and Their Treatment: An Outline," *International Journal of Psychoanalysis* 59 (1978): 414. Read also Pamela Cooper-White, *Many Voices: Pastoral Psychotherapy in Relational and Theological Perspective* (Minneapolis, MN: Fortress Press, 2007), 111, where she discusses Ernest Wolf and others who built on Kohut's initial selfobject-transference experiences to identify a total of six selfobject-transferences: mirroring, idealizing, twinship, alter ego, adversarial, and companion. For the purposes of this discussion, analysis is limited to mirroring and idealizing selfobject and cultural selfobject experiences.

16. To be clear, the splitting defenses and adaptive behaviors related to narcissistic wounding are similar in their presentation; however, they are not the same as splitting defenses enacted in posttraumatic splitting following intimate violence. Although narcissistic wounds are related to empathically failing nurturing contexts that can impact character/personality formation, they may or may not also include traumatic encounters like childhood neglect, sexual and/or physical abuse. Classic narcissistic wounds are related to events and experiences that occur between zero and three years of age, at a time when intrapsychic core formation is taking place. They come about as a result of experiences that force the enactment of intrapsychic defenses (disavowal, dissociation, repression) that become organizing elements in the intrapsychic core. When working with people who experienced sexual, physical, or emotional abuse in the early stages of development, the transference that develops between client and care provider should be viewed as evidence of traumatic events that have become part of the individual's personality organization.

   If a painful and/or traumatic event occurs at a later stage in intrapsychic development, the defenses should be understood primarily as symptoms of posttraumatic stress disorder, which is similar in its presentation, but may be different in its origin from narcissistic wounding. This would be the case for someone who was abused in later adolescence or adulthood and whose intra- and interpersonal encounters are marked by dissociation and repression. In these cases, the defenses are not a part of their core characterological formation.

17. Sheppard, *Self, Culture and Others in Womanist Practical Theology,* 113.

18. Ibid., 56.

19. Heinz Kohut, *Self Psychology and the Humanities: Reflections on a New Psychoanalytic Approach* (New York: W. W. Norton & Company, 1985), 227.

20. Ibid.

21. Sheppard, *Self, Culture and Others in Womanist Practical Theology*, 121–122.

22. Ibid., 115.

23. Toni Morrison, *What Moves at the Margins: Selected Nonfiction* (Jackson: University of Mississippi, 2008), 200.

24. Read Emilie M. Townes, "To Pick One's Own Cotton: Religious Values, Public Policy and Women's Moral Autonomy," in *Womanist Ethics and the Cultural Production of Evil* (New York: Palgrave Macmillan, 2006), chapter 6, 111–138, where Townes analyzes the political consequences of sexual mythologies on US public policy decisions that revolve around depictions of Black women's sexual and moral agency and in turn negatively impact access to resources and quality of life.

25. Brown Douglas, *Sexuality and the Black Church*.

26. Ibid., 118.

27. Ibid., 116.

28. Cooper-White, *Many Voices*, 41.

29. Sheppard, *Self, Culture and Others*, 187.

30. Williams, *Sisters in the Wilderness*.

31. Ibid., 162.

32. Ibid., 163.

33. Ibid., 164.

34. Monica, A. Coleman, *Making a Way Out of No Way: A Postmodern Womanist Theology* (Minneapolis, MN: Fortress Press, 2008), 93.

35. Williams, *Sisters in the Wilderness*, 166.

36. All names have been changed to protect the identity of participants in the research study. Additionally, names of identifying cities, institutions, and friends or relatives of participants have been omitted or altered to ensure anonymity.

1   I Can Speak (the Unspeakable) for Myself

1. All names have been changed to protect the identities of participants in the research study. In addition I have omitted or altered the names of identifying cities, institutions, friends and relatives of participants to ensure anonymity.

2. Iyanla Vanzant, *One Day My Soul Just Opened up: 40 Days and Nights towards Spiritual Strength and Personal Growth* (New York: Fireside Books, 1998).

3. Susan L. Taylor, *In the Spirit: Inspirational Writings of Susan L. Taylor* (New York: Amistad, 1999).

2   Navigating the Hostile Terrain of Intimate and Cultural Violence

1. Phillis I. Sheppard, *Self, Culture and Others in Womanist Practical Theology* (New York: Palgrave Macmillan, 2011), 117–118. For the purposes of this research, analysis focuses on mirroring and idealizing self-object and cultural selfobject experiences. Read Pamela Cooper-White, *Many Voices: Pastoral Psychotherapy in Relational and Theological Perspective* (Minneapolis, MN: Fortress Press, 2007), 111, for discussion of other selfobject experiences including twinship, alter ego, adversarial, and companion.
2. Laura S. Josephs, "The Treatment of an Adult Survivor of Incest: A Self psychological Perspective," *American Journal of Psychoanalysis* 52 (1992): 210.
3. Ibid., 203.
4. Judith Herman, *Trauma and Recovery: The Aftermath of Violence: From Domestic Abuse to Political Terror* (New York: Basic Books, 1992), 110–111.
5. Heinz Kohut, "The Disorders of the Self and Their Treatment: An Outline," *International Journal of Psychoanalysis* 59 (1978): 417.
6. Patricia Hill Collins, *Black Feminist Thought: Knowledge, Consciousness and the Politics of Empowerment* (New York: Routledge, 2000).
7. Ibid., 178.
8. Tracy Robinson and Janie Victoria Ward, "A Belief in Self Far Greater Than Anyone's Disbelief: Cultivating Resistance Among African American Female Adolescents," in *Girls, Women and Psychotherapy: Reframing Resistance*, ed. Carol Gilligan, Annie G. Rogers, and Deborah L. Tolman (Binghamton, NY: Harrington Park Press, 1991), 87–103, quoted in Phillis I. Sheppard, *Self, Culture and Others*, 118–119.
9. Heinz Kohut, *Self Psychology and the Humanities: Reflections on a New Psychoanalytic Approach* (New York: W. W. Norton & Company, 1985), 227.
10. Rosalyn M. Story, *And So I Sing: African American Divas of Opera and Concert* (New York: Harper Collins, 2000).
11. Sheppard, *Self, Culture and Others*, 115.
12. Ibid., 114, Sheppard quoting Kohut and Wolf, "Disorders of the Self and Their Treatment: An Outline," 177.

3   A God I Recognize

1. See Tracey E. Hucks, *Yoruba Traditions and African American Religious Nationalism* (New Mexico: University of New Mexico Press, 2012), for a detailed discussion of African American engagement of Yoruba religion and its derivative forms as a religious tradition to which many

African Americans are drawn as an expression of their allegiance to African heritage, spirituality, culture, and as resistance against Western hegemony.

2. See Marita Golden's "The Power of Affirmations," in *My Soul Is a Witness: African American Women's Spirituality,* ed. Gloria Wade-Gayles (Boston: Beacon Press, 1995), 338. Golden describes affirmations as a form or prayer that invites the speaker to actively participate in the fulfilment of the prayer.

> I have been composing affirmations for the past five years as a form of prayer. Unlike some who see affirmations as distinctly different in intent and nature than the ritual of prayer, for me the affirmations are simply another form or type of prayer. Like prayers, affirmations are an invitation for the world to manifest in benevolent ways. I use affirmations not so much to try to control reality (which is impossible anyway), as to feel and tap into the power of love and to feel a connectedness with the Ultimate Power. Affirmations allow me to acknowledge that I am not alone, even in moments of crisis, doubt or confusion, that I can and do believe in my value and in God's benevolence. Affirmations state in a powerful, totally fulfilling way that I am God's eyes, hands, ears, legs and mind on earth and lead me always, relentlessly, and certainly back to love, forgiveness and understanding of myself and others. But affirmations possess their unique power in tandem with the organic, whole nature and personality of one's life. Affirmations must echo and reflect the choices and decisions made and sought during the mundane, often trying minutes, hour, day and weeks of every life. Whatever power affirmations possess is acquired through weaving their spirit throughout the texture of one's dreams and desires and yearnings. Affirmations have helped me to change my life and shape new values, have given me courage and led me to peace of mind.

3. Iyanla Vanzant, *One Day My Soul Just Opened up: 40 Days and Nights towards Spiritual Strength and Personal Growth* (New York: Fireside Books, 1998).

4. Ibid., 180.

5. Kelly Brown Douglas, *Sexuality and the Black Church: A Womanist Perspective* (Maryknoll, NY: Orbis Books, 2003).

6. Delores S. Williams, *Sisters in the Wilderness: The Challenge of Womanist God-Talk* (Maryknoll, NY: Orbis Books, 2004), 142.

7. Douglas, *Sexuality and the Black Church,* 118.

8. Williams, *Sisters in the Wilderness,* 161–162.

9. Williams writes about defilement as meaning "to ravish, violate...to sully, dishonor" in her chapter, "A Womanist Perspective on Sin," in *A Troubling in My Soul: Womanist Perspectives on Evil and Suffering,* ed. Emilie M. Townes (Maryknoll, NY: Orbis Books, 1993), 144.

10. I borrow the term "defilement" from Phillis Sheppard's use of it to describe the spiritual implications of violence. In *Self, Culture and Others: A Womanist Practical Theology* (New York: Palgrave Macmillan, 2012), 17–18, she builds on initial thoughts formulated by Delores S. Williams to clarify how intimate and cultural violence are not simply interpersonal actions; they also have a spiritual component in that the acts ignore and refute God's initial declaration that each individual is made in God's own image, and is thus worthy of treatment that reflects this ontological truth.

11. Williams, *Sisters in the Wilderness*, 162.

4   WomanistCare: Reshaping Images and Paradigms for Care

1. See Marsha Foster Boyd, "WomanistCare," in *Embracing the Spirit: Womanist Perspectives on Hope, Salvation, and Transformation*, ed. Emilie M. Townes (Maryknoll, NY: Orbis, 1997), 199.

2. Caroll Watkins Ali, *Survival and Liberation: Pastoral Theology in African American Context* (St. Louis, MO: Chalice Press, 1999), 120.

3. Ibid., 120.

4. For more Womanist and Feminist analysis of norms and paradigms for care, see Bonnie J. Miller-McClemore and Brita Gill-Austern, eds., *Feminist and Womanist Pastoral Theology* (Nashville, TN: Abingdon, 1999); Nancy J. Gorsuch, *Introducing Feminist Pastoral Care and Counseling* (Cleveland, OH: The Pilgrim Press, 2001); Nancy J. Ramsay, ed., *Pastoral Care and Counseling: Redefining the Paradigms* (Nashville, TN: Abingdon Press, 2004); Jeanne Stevenson-Moessner and Teresa Snorton, eds., *Women Out of Order: Risking Change and Creating Care in a Multicultural World* (Minneapolis: Fortress Press, 2010); Chanequa Walker Barnes, *Too Heavy a Yoke: Black Women and the Burden of Strength* (Eugene, OR: Wipf and Stock, 2014).

5. Major voices include Linda H. Hollies, ed., *WomanistCare: How to Tend the Souls of Women, Volume 1* (Evanston, IL: Woman to Woman Ministries, Inc., 1992); Teresa Snorton, "The Legacy of the African American Matriarch: New Perspectives for Pastoral Care," in *Through the Eyes of Women: Insights For Pastoral Care*, ed. Jeanne Stevenson Moessner (Minneapolis: Fortress Press, 1996), 50–56; Beverly Wallace, "A Womanist Legacy of Trauma, Grief and Loss: Reframing the Notion of the Strong Black Woman Icon," in *Women Out of Order: Risking Change in a Multicultural World*, ed. Jeanne Stevenson Moessner and Teresa Snorton (Minneapolis, MN: Fortress Press, 2009) 43–56; Elizabeth Johnson Walker, "Counseling Grace: A Pastoral Theology," in *Women Out of Order: Risking Change in a Multicultural World*, ed. Jeanne Stevenson Moessner and Teresa Snorton (Minneapolis,

MN: Fortress Press, 2009), 243–254. And, most recently, Phillis I. Sheppard, *Self, Culture and Others in Womanist Practical Theology* (New York: Palgrave Macmillan, 2012). Read especially, Sheppard, "The Current Shape of Womanist Practical Theology," Chapter 3, in *Self, Culture and Other*, for a discussion and critique of contemporary Womanist scholarship on the applicability of psychodynamic theory with African American women. These books, articles, and essays are seminal Womanist deconstructions of cultural norms that undergird ideas about the form and function of pastoral theology, care and counseling, and their implications for African American women.

6. The definition I offer here of cultural countertransference builds on an analysis Emmanuel Y. Lartey presents in his discussion of intercultural pastoral counseling. In *In Living Color: An Intercultural Approach to Pastoral Counseling,* 2nd Edition (London: Jessica Kingsley Press, 2003), 32, Lartey observes, "…stereotyping is a particularly neurotic form of reductionism, in which, as a result of an inability to cope with complexity or difference, an attempt is made to control by placing groups in hierarchical order, categorizing them and seeing any particular individual member of a particular group as bearing the presumed characteristics of that group." The ubiquitous nature of stereotypes requires self-awareness of how these stereotypes are present even in the most well-meaning persons.

7. Toni Morrison, *Beloved* (New York: Alfred A. Knopf, 2004).

8. See also Edward P. Wimberly, *African American Pastoral Counseling: The Politics of Oppression and Empowerment* (Cleveland, OH: Pilgrim, 2006).

9. See also Teresa L. Fry Brown's *God Don't Like Ugly: African American Women Handing on Spiritual Values* (Nashville, TN: Abingdon Press, 2000), where she discusses literature, film, music, and visual arts as creative mediums through which African Americans transfer knowledge and wisdom intergenerationally.

10. Craig Dykstra, *Images of Pastoral Care: Classic Readings* (St. Louis, Missouri: Chalice Press, 2005).

11. See Stevenson–Moessner and Snorton's *Women out of Order* for emergent voices who take up this challenge. In particular, read Michelle Oberwise Lacock and Carol Lakota Eastin, "We Hold Our Stories in Blankets: Pastoral Care with American Indian Women," 93–114; and, Adriana P. Cavina, "La Veglia: Keeping Vigil: The Power of Storytelling and Story Sharing in Women's Lives; A Study of Mediterranean Culture," 149–158.

12. African American clinical pastoral education (CPE) supervisor and former executive director of the Association for Clinical Pastoral Education, Teresa Snorton, writes about training resources she developed to support Black female CPE students, and to inform non-Black CPE students and supervisors about the impact of stereotypes on clinical training contexts.

See her article, "What about All Those Angry Black Women," in the volume she co-edited with Jeanne Stevenson Moessner, *Women out of Order: Risking Change and Creating Care in a Multicultural World.*

13. Morrison, *Beloved,* 103.

14. Morrison, *Beloved,* 104–105.

15. See also Lee H. Butler Jr., "African American Spirituality as Survival," in *Liberating Our Dignity, Saving Our Souls* (Danvers, MA: Chalice Press, 2006), Chapter 7, 104–118.

16. See Katie Cannon, "Moral Wisdom in the Black Women's Literary Tradition," Chapter 4; and "Resources for a Constructive Ethic: The Life and Work of Zora Neale Hurston," Chapter 6, in *Katie's Canon: Womanism and the Soul of the Black Community* (New York: Continuum, 1995) for a thorough discussion of the role of African American women writers in contributing narratives about African American moral wisdom, including spirituality.

17. Toni Morrison, "The Site of Memory," in *Inventing the Truth: The Art and Craft of Memoir,* rev. and exp., ed. William Zinsser (Boston, MA: Houghton, Mifflin Company, 1998), 186.

18. Foster Boyd, "WomanistCare," 200.

19. Ibid.

20. Malidoma Patrice Somé, *The Healing Wisdom of Africa: Finding Life Purpose through Nature, Ritual and Community* (New York: Jeremy P. Tarcher/Putnam, 1999), 141.

21. See Monica A. Coleman, "Learning from the Past: The Role of the Ancestors," in *Making a Way Out of No Way: A Womanist Theology* (Minneapolis, MN: Fortress Press, 2008), Chapter 4, 101, where she writes, "Womanist theologies remind us that black women have histories with experiences of violence and destruction. Womanist theologies discuss the ways that black women find resources for survival and life in their spiritual and cultural pasts. The postmodern theological framework acknowledges that every move into the future entails some loss of what we once experienced. Nevertheless, there are ways that the past remains alive to us today. We can creatively transform the past to decide how we should move into the future. We can also draw power from the lives of those who have come before us, as we learn from the past, our ancestors have their own kind of immortality." To further explain the moral implications of a spirituality that includes active engagement with ancestors, on page 114 she quotes African Religions scholar Jacob K. Olupona, "In order to function [as guardians of moral authority], the ancestors are freed of the human weaknesses and conditions of pettiness, particularly common among living lineage members. They are, therefore, eminently qualified to act as the guardians of social and moral order."

22. James L. Griffith and Mellissa Elliott Griffith, *Encountering The Sacred in Psychotherapy: How to Talk to People about Their Spiritual Lives* (New York: Guilford Press, 2003), 167.

23. For more information on First Afrikan Presbyterian Church, visit them online at www.FirstAfrikanChurch.org.

24. In addition to providing ministerial leadership at First Afrikan, Itihari Toure, EdD, is also director of the Black Women in Ministry (BWIM) Leadership Development program in the Office of Black Women in Church and Society founded by first-generation Womanist Jacquelyn Grant. Toure's theological framework for working with the women in the BWIM program, as well as her work with the women in the community, is informed by doctoral research on African-centered communal collective models of transformation, as well as a master's level research in human development.

25. In Yoruba religious tradition, when the Creator God calls forth life in human form, the individual receives her or his Ase´, *a* sacred identity and purpose given to him/her by Spirit. Saying Ase´ each time an ancestor's name is called is the community's way of asking ancestors to offer up the best of their Ase´ as a guiding force that helps the living community recall and live into its identity and collective purpose. In *Making a Way Out of No Way: A Womanist Theology,* Womanist theologian Monica A. Coleman writes about how Black Christianity has historically incorporated African religious retentions like Yoruba belief and culture into its identity. Read page 109 where Coleman notes, "Through both the triangular slave trade and contemporary reversionist attempts at recapturing traditional religions, the religion of the Yoruba people (of current-day Nigeria) has constituted a base for African-derived religious practices throughout the Caribbean, South America, and the United States." On page 112 she clarifies, "When speaking of the presence of traditional Yoruba religion in the United States, one must also include contemporary revisionist attempts to reclaim cultural identity through an intentional revival of and return to ancient traditions. Practitioners will often refer to this system of belief and practices as "Ifa" or "Yoruba." For a further discussion of Yoruba religion in America, see Tracey E. Hucks, *Yoruba and African American Religious Nationalism* (New Mexico: University of New Mexico Press, 2012).

26. Ifa religious leaders are both women and men who are responsible for maintaining the wisdom and content of the tradition through myths, songs, and the Odu, sacred texts of wisdom and divination. One of the ways that First Afrikan embodied its commitment to "re-formation of Christianity ministry in the United States" involved creating space to include religious leaders who offer insight from African traditional religions to the sacred space of worship and liturgy, like Ifa priestess Eniola Kalimara's participation in the eight bowl ritual.

27. The description of the significance of the elements described here may be found in Askhari Johnson Hodari's *The African Book of Names: 5,000 Common and Uncommon Names from the African Continent*

(Deerfield Beach, FL: Health Communications, Inc., 2009). In the text Hodari notes that while the ritual and elements are described in her text for the purposes of their inclusion in a baby-naming ceremony, the same elements have been used to mark other significant life passages. Toure adapted the ritual to address the pastoral needs she observed for a ritual acknowledging significant events and experiences in the lives of the women at the First Afrikan church and the surrounding community.

28. Itihari Toure, telephone conversation with author, February 18, 2012.
29. Jan Berry, "Whose Threshold? Women's Strategies of Ritualization," *Feminist Theology* 14 (2006): 287, referencing Heather Walton, "Speaking in Signs: Narrative and Trauma in Pastoral Theology," *Scottish Journal of Health Care Chaplaincy* 5 (2002): 2.
30. See "Power and Violence against Women," in Pamela Cooper-White, *The Rape of Tamar: Violence against Women and the Church's Response, 2nd Edition* (Minneapolis, MN: Fortress Press, 1995) Chapter 1. Cooper-White examines existing definitions to provide a baseline understanding of what is meant when the term "power" is used. Building on early feminist analysis, she revisits a popular threefold typology of power: "Power over" (the power of dominion over others), "power within" (the power of one's own inner wisdom, intuition, self-esteem, even the spark of the divine), and "power with" (the power of an individual to reach out in a manner that negates neither self nor other). Cooper-White critiques the third dimension of this typology. Rather than "power with," on page 59 she suggests an understanding of "power-within community" to articulate a third dimension of power that "embraces the power of the individual self and values relationality and mutuality but also is large enough to meet the challenges of the larger sphere of social construction."
31. Gail E. Wyatt, Jennifer Vargas Carmona, Tamra Burns Loeb, Armida Ayala, and Dorothy Chin, "Sexual Abuse," in *Handbook of Women's Sexual and Reproductive Health*, ed. Gina M. Wingood and Ralph J. DiClemente (New York: Kluwer Academic/Plenum Publishers, 2002), 201.
32. Marie M. Fortune and James Newton Poling, "Calling to Accountability: The Church's Response to Abusers," in *Violence against Women: A Christian Theological Sourcebook*, ed. Carol J. Adams and Marie M. Fortune (New York: Continuum, 1995), 455.
33. Nicholas Groth, *Men Who Rape* (New York: Plenum, 1979), 4, quoted in Marie Fortune and James Newton Poling, "Calling to Accountability: The Church's Response to Abusers," in *Violence against Women and Children: A Christian Theological Sourcebook*, ed. Carol J. Adams and Marie M. Fortune (New York: Continuum, 1995), 455.
34. Fortune and Poling, "Calling to Accountability," 456.

5 Womanist Pastoral Counseling: Clinical Considerations

1. Pamela Cooper-White, *The Cry of Tamar*, 2nd Edition (Minneapolis: Fortress Press, 2012).
2. Ibid., 183–184.
3. Ibid., 118.
4. Ibid., 117–118.
5. Ibid., 141.
6. Judith Herman, *Trauma and Recovery: The Aftermath of Violence: From Domestic Abuse to Political Terror* (New York: Basic Books, 1992).
7. Ibid., 36.
8. Ibid., 37.
9. Ibid., 43.
10. Ibid., 47.
11. Ibid., 47.
12. Ibid., 47.
13. Ibid., 136.
14. Ibid., 136–137.
15. See Pamela Cooper-White, *Many Voices: Pastoral Psychotherapy in Relational and Theological Perspective* (Minneapolis: Fortress Press, 2007); Phillis I. Sheppard, *Self, Culture and Others in Womanist Practical Theology* (New York: Palgrave Macmillan, 2011); and, Christie Cozad Neuger, *Counseling Women: A Narrative Counseling Approach to Pastoral Care* (Minneapolis, MN: Fortress Press, 2001).
16. Neuger, 37.
17. Carolyn A. L. McCrary, "Intimate Violence against Black Women," *Journal of the Interdenominational Theological Center*, No. 28 (Fall 1998).
18. See Marie A. Fortune, *Sexual Violence: The Sin Revisited* (Cleveland, OH: The Pilgrim Press, 2005), 145–146, where she considers the particularity of shame in Christian women who are healing from intimate violence. "For victim/survivors who are Christians, there may be additional feelings of guilt and shame stemming from religious teachings...If a woman accepts the Christian teaching that sexual activity outside of marriage is sinful and that women are seductive temptresses, then she will probably view her victimization as a sexual sin and see herself as being responsible."
19. See Melissa V. Harris-Perry, "Myth," in *Sister Citizen: Shame, Stereotypes and Black Women in America* (New Haven, CT, and London: Yale University Press, 2011), Chapter 2, 97.
20. Fortune, *Sexual Violence*, 31.
21. McCrary, "Intimate Violence," 15.
22. Ibid., 15–16.

23. Pamela Cooper-White, *Many Voices: Pastoral Psychotherapy in Relational and Theological Perspective* (Minneapolis: Fortress Press, 2007), 117.

24. bell hooks, *Sisters of the Yam: Black Women and Self Recovery* (Cambridge: South End Press, 1999), 22.

25. Darlene Clark-Hine, "Rape and the Inner Lives of Black Women in the Midwest," *Signs* 14, no. 4 (Summer 1998): 912–920.

26. Heinz Kohut, "On Empathy," *International Journal of Psychoanalytic Self Psychology* 5 (2011): 126.

27. Ibid., 128.

28. Fortune, *Sexual Violence,* 163. See also, 251–262, in Cooper-White, *The Cry of Tamar,* for discussion on "remembering," "self forgiveness," "letting go," and "reconciliation" as components that, when taken together, support possibilities for forgiving intimate violence.

29. See Phillis I. Sheppard, "Mourning the Loss of Cultural Selfobjects: Black Embodiment and Religious Experience after Trauma," *Practical Theology* 1, no. 2 (2008): 1–20. See also McCrary, "Intimate Violence against Black Women," 5–6, for her discussion of the community's role and responsibility to join Black women in public, communal practices of lament that lead to individual and collective healing; and Herman, "Remembrance and Mourning," Chapter 9, 175–196, in *Trauma and Recovery.*

30. Sheppard, "Mourning the Loss of Cultural Selfobjects," 22–23, quoting Martha R. Fowlkes, "The Morality of Loss: The Social Construction of Mourning and Melancholia," *Contemporary Psychoanalysis,* 27 (1991): 532.

Conclusion

1. Toni Morrison, *Beloved* (New York: Alfred A. Knopf, 2004), 104.

2. Carolyn Yoder, *The Little Book of Trauma Healing* (Intercourse, PA: Good Books, 2005), 14.

Bibliography

Berry, Jan. "Whose Threshold? Women's Strategies of Ritualization." *Feminist Theology* 14 (2006): 273–288.

Black, Michele C., Kathleen C. Basile, Matthew J. Breiding, Sharon G. Smith, Mikel L. Walters, Melissa T. Merrick, Jieru Chen, and Mark R. Stevens. National Center for Injury Prevention and Control, Centers for Disease Control and Prevention. *The National Intimate Partner and Sexual Violence Survey (NISVS): 2010 Summary Report* (2011). http://www.cdc.gov/violenceprevention/pdf/nisvs_report2010-a.pdf, accessed January 20, 2014.

Boyd-Franklin, Nancy. *Black Families in Therapy: Understanding the African American Experience,* 2nd Edition. New York: The Guilford Press, 2003.

Butler Jr., Lee H. *Liberating Our Dignity, Saving Our Souls.* Danvers, MA: Chalice Press, 2006.

Canon, Katie G. "Hitting a Straight Lick with a Crooked Stick: The Womanist Dilemma in the Development of a Black Liberation Ethic." *Annual of the Society of Christian Ethics* (1987):165–177.

———. *Katie's Canon: Womanism and the Soul of the Black Community.* New York: Continuum, 1995.

Chung, Hyun Kyung. *Struggle to Be the Sun Again: Asian Women's Theology.* Maryknoll, NY: Orbis Books, 1990.

Clark-Hine, Darlene. "Rape and the Inner Lives of Black Women in the Midwest." *Signs* 14, no. 4 (Summer 1998): 912–920.

Coleman, Monica A. *The Dinah Project: A Handbook for Congregational Response to Sexual Violence.* Cleveland, OH: Pilgrim Press, 2004.

———. *Making a Way Out of No Way: A Womanist Theology.* Minneapolis, MN: Fortress Press, 2008.

Collins, Patricia Hill. *Black Feminist Thought: Knowledge, Consciousness and the Politics of Empowerment.* New York: Routledge, 2000.

———. *Black Sexual Politics: African Americans, Gender and the New Racism.* New York: Routledge, 2004.

Cooper-White, Pamela. *Many Voices: Pastoral Psychotherapy in Relational and Theological Perspective.* Minneapolis, MN: Fortress Press, 2007.

Cooper-White, Pamela. *The Cry of Tamar: Violence against Women and the Church's Response.* 2nd Edition. Minneapolis, MN: Fortress Press, 2012.

Creswell, John W. *Qualitative Inquiry and Research Design: Choosing among Five Traditions.* Thousand Oaks, CA: Sage Publications, 2007.

Crisp, Beth R. "Spirituality and Sexual Abuse: Issues and Dilemmas for Survivors." *Theology and Sexuality* 13, no. 3 (2007): 301–314.

DeGruchy, Steven, Sinatra Matimelo, and Jim Olivier. "Participatory Inquiry on the Interface between Religion and Health: What Does It Achieve, and What Not?" Plenary Address, Maps and Mazes: Critical Inquiry at the Intersection of Religion and Health Conference, Atlanta, GA, November 2007.

Douglas, Kelly Brown. *Sexuality and the Black Church: A Womanist Perspective.* Maryknoll, NY: Orbis Books, 2003.

Dykstra, Craig. *Images of Pastoral Care: Classic Readings.* St. Louis, MO: Chalice Press, 2005.

Eugene, Toinette M. "While Love Is Unfashionable: Ethical Implications of Black Spirituality and Sexuality." In *Sexuality and the Sacred: Sources for Theological Reflection,* edited by James B. Nelson and Sandra P. Longfellow, 105–114. Louisville, KY: Westminster John Knox Press, 1994.

———. "Swing Low Sweet Chariot: A Womanist Ethical Response to Sexual Violence and Abuse." In *Violence against Women: A Theological Sourcebook,* edited by Marie M. Fortune and Carol J. Adams, 185–200. New York: Continuum, 1995.

———. "Lifting as We Climb, Womanist Theorizing about Religion and the Family." In *Religion, Feminism and the Family,* edited by Anne E. Carr and Mary Stewart Van Leeuwen, 330–343. New York: Westminster John Knox, 1996.

Eugene, Toinette M. and James N. Poling. *Balm for Gilead: Pastoral Care for African American Families Experiencing Abuse.* Nashville, TN: Abingdon, 1998.

Few, April L., Dionne P. Stephens, and Mario Rouse-Arnett. "Sister-to-Sister Talk: Transcending Boundaries and Challenges in Qualitative Research with Black Women." *Family Relations* 52, no. 3 (2003): 205–215.

Fortune, Marie M. *Sexual Violence: The Unmentionable Sin.* Cleveland, OH: Pilgrim Press: 1983.

———. "The Way Things Are Is Not the Way They Have to Be." In *Sexuality and the Sacred: Sources for Theological Reflection,* edited by James B. Nelson and Sandra P. Longfellow, 326–334. Louisville, KY: Westminster John Knox Press, 1994.

———. *Sexual Violence: The Sin Revisited.* Cleveland, OH: Pilgrim Press, 2005.

Fortune, Marie and Carol J. Adams, eds. *Violence against Women: A Theological Sourcebook.* New York: Continuum, 1995.

Foster-Boyd. "WomanistCare." In *Embracing the Spirit: Womanist Perspectives on Hope, Salvation, and Transformation,* edited by Emilie M. Townes, 197–202. Maryknoll, NY: Orbis, 1997.

Fry Brown, Teresa L. *God Don't Like Ugly: African American Women Handing on Spiritual Values.* Nashville, TN: Abingdon Press, 2000.

Gilkes, Cheryl Townsend. "The 'Loves' and the 'Troubles' of African American Women's Bodies: The Womanist Challenge to Cultural Humiliation and Community Ambivalence." In *A Troubling in My Soul: Womanist Perspectives on Evil and Suffering,* edited by Emilie M. Townes, Chapter 14, 232–249. Maryknoll, NY: Orbis Books, 1993.

Goldberg, Arnold and Paul Stepansky, eds. *How Does Analysis Cure? Heinz Kohut.* Chicago, IL: University of Chicago Press, 1984.

Golden, Marita. "The Power of Affirmations." In *My Soul Is a Witness: African American Women's Spirituality,* edited by Gloria Wade-Gayles, 338–340. Boston, MA: Beacon Press, 1995.

Gorsuch, Nancy J. *Introducing Feminist Pastoral Care and Counseling.* Cleveland, OH: Pilgrim Press, 2001.

Graham, Elaine. "Practical Theology as Transforming Practice." In *The Blackwell Reader in Pastoral and Practical Theology,* edited by James Woodward and Stephen Pattison, 104–117. Malden, MA: Blackwell Publishing, 2000.

Graham, Larry Kent. *Care of Persons, Care of Worlds: A Psychosystems Approach to Pastoral Care and Counseling.* Nashville, TN: Abingdon, 1992.

Grant, Jacquelyn A. *White Women's Christ and Black Women's Jesus: Feminist Christology and Womanist Response.* Atlanta, GA: Scholars Press, 1999.

———. "The Sin of Servanthood and the Deliverance of Discipleship." In *A Troubling in My Soul: Womanist Perspectives on Evil and Suffering,* edited by Emilie M. Townes, 199–218. Maryknoll, NY: Orbis Books, 1993.

Griffith, James L. and Mellissa Elliott Griffith. *Encountering the Sacred in Psychotherapy: How to Talk to People About Their Spiritual Lives.* New York: Guilford Press, 2003.

Hadad, Beverly and Stephen De Gruchy. "Mapping Religious Health Assets," in *The Potential and Perils of Partnership: Christian Religious Entities and Collaborative Stakeholders Responding to HIV and Aids in Kenya, Malawi, and the DRC* (2008), Chapter 2. http://www.arhap.uct.ac.za/downloads/ARHAPWHO_ch2.pdf.

Hanna, Judith Lynn. "Marian Chace Foundation Annual Lecture: October 2005 The Power of Dance Discourse, Explanation in Self Defense." *American Journal of Dance Therapy* 28, no. 1 (Spring/Summer 2006): 3–19.

Herman, Judith. *Trauma and Recovery: The Aftermath of Violence—from Domestic Abuse to Political Terror.* New York: Basic Books, 1980.

Higginbotham, Evelyn Brooks. *Righteous Discontent: The Women's Movement in the Black Baptist Church, 1880–1920*. Boston, MA: Harvard University Press, 1994.

Hodari, Askhari Johnson. *The African Book of Names: 5,000 Common and Uncommon Names from the African Continent*. Deerfield Beach, FL: Health Communications, Inc., 2009.

Hollies, Linda M. "When the Mountain Won't Move." In *Violence against Women: A Theological Sourcebook*, edited by Marie M. Fortune and Carol J. Adams, 314–327. New York: Continuum, 1995.

———, ed. *WomanistCare: How to Tend the Souls of Women*, Volume 1. Jackson, Michigan: Woman to Woman Ministries, Inc., 1992.

Harris-Perry, Melissa V. *Sister Citizen: Shame, Stereotypes and Black Women in America*. New Haven, CT, and London: Yale University Press, 2011.

hooks, bell. *Sisters of the Yam: Black Women and Self Recovery*. Cambridge: South End Press, 1999.

Hopkins, Dwight N. *Down, Up and Over: Slave Religion and Black Theology*. Minneapolis, MN: Fortress Press, 2000.

———. *Being Human: Race, Religion and Culture*. Minneapolis, MN: Augsburg Press, 2005.

Hopkins, Dwight N. and Anthony B. Pinn, eds. *Loving the Body: Black Religious Studies and the Erotic*. New York: Palgrave Macmillan, 2004.

Hucks, Tracey E. *Yoruba and African American Religious Nationalism*. New Mexico: University of New Mexico Press, 2012.

Jackson, Leslie C. and Beverly Greene, eds. *Psychotherapy with African American Women: Innovations in Psychodynamic Perspectives and Practice*. London/New York: The Guilford Press, 2000.

Josephs, Laura S. "The Treatment of an Adult Survivor of Incest: A Self Psychological Perspective." *American Journal of Psychoanalysis* 52 (1992): 201–212.

Kohut, Heinz. *Restoration of the Self*. Connecticut: International Universities Press, 1977.

———. *Self Psychology and the Humanities: Reflections on a New Psychoanalytic Approach*. Edited by Charles B. Strozier. New York: W. W. Norton & Company, 1985.

———. "On Empathy." *International Journal of Psychoanalytic Self Psychology* 5 (2010): 122–131.

Kohut, Heinz and Ernest Wolf. "The Disorders of the Self and Their Treatment: An Outline." *International Journal of Psychoanalysis* 59 (1978): 414–425.

Lartey, Emmanuel Y. *In Living Color: An Intercultural Approach to Pastoral Care and Counseling*, 2nd Edition. London and Philadelphia, PA: Jessica Kingsley Publishers, 2003.

Lorde, Audre. *Sister Outsider: Essays and Speeches by Audre Lorde*. Berkeley, CA: The Crossing Press, 1984.

Manlowe, Jennifer L. "Seduced by Faith: Sexual Traumas and Their Embodied Effects." In *Violence against Women: A Theological Sourcebook*, edited by Marie M. Fortune and Carol J. Adams, 328–338. New York: Continuum, 1995.

McCrary, Carolyn A. L. "Interdependence as a Normative Value in Pastoral Counseling with African Americans." In *Recovery of Black Presence, An Interdisciplinary Exploration: Essays in Honor of Charles B. Copher*, edited by Randall Bailey and Jacquelyn Grant, 159–175. Nashville, TN: Abingdon Press, 1995.

———. "The Wholeness of Women." *Journal of the Interdenominational Theological Center* 25 (June 1998): 258–294.

———. "Intimate Violence against Black Women." *Journal of the Interdenominational Theological Center* 28 (Fall 1998): 3–37.

Miller-McLemore, Bonnie J. "How Sexuality and Relationships Have Revolutionized Pastoral Theology." In *The Blackwell Reader in Practical and Pastoral Theology*, edited by James Woodard and Stephen Pattison, 233–247. Malden, MA: Blackwell Publishing, 2000.

Miller-McLemore, Bonnie J. and Brita Gill Austern, eds. *Feminist and Womanist Pastoral Theology*. Nashville, TN: Abingdon, 1999.

Mitchem, Stephanie Y. *African American Folk Healing*. New York: New York University Press, 2007.

Moessner, Jeanne Stevenson., ed. *Through the Eyes of Women: Insights for Pastoral Care*. Minneapolis MN: Fortress Press, 1996.

Moessner, Jeanne Stevenson and Teresa A. Snorton, eds. *Women out of Order: Risking Change and Creating Care in a Multicultural World*. Minneapolis, MN: Fortress Press, 2010.

Morrison, Toni. "The Site of Memory." In *Inventing the Truth: The Art and Craft of Memoir*, rev. and exp., edited by William Zinsser, 183–200. Boston, MA: Houghton, Mifflin Company, 1998.

———. *Beloved* (New York: Alfred A. Knopf, 2004).

———. *What Moves at the Margins: Selected Nonfiction*. Jackson, Mississippi: University of Mississippi, 2008.

Moschella, Mary Clark. *Ethnography as a Pastoral Practice: An Introduction*. Cleveland, OH: Pilgrim Press, 2008.

Nakashima Brock, Rita. *Theologies by Heart: A Christology of Erotic Power*. New York: The Crossroad Publishing Company, 1988.

Neuger, Christie Cozad. *Counseling Women: A Narrative Pastoral Approach*. Minneapolis, MN: Augsburg Fortress Press, 2001.

Poling, James N. *The Abuse of Power: A Theological Problem*. Nashville, TN: Abingdon, 1991.

Ramsay, Nancy J. *Pastoral Counseling: Redefining the Paradigms*. Nashville, TN: Abingdon Press, 2004.

Robinson, Tracy and Janie Victoria Ward, "A Belief in Self Far Greater Than Anyone's Disbelief: Cultivating Resistance among African American Female Adolescents." In *Girls, Women and Psychotherapy: Reframing*

Resistance, edited by . Carol Gilligan, Annie G. Rogers, and Deborah L. Tolman, 87–103. Binghamton, NY: Harrington Park, Press, 1991.

Sheppard, Phillis I. "No Rose-Colored Glasses: Womanist Practical Theology and Response to Sexual Violence." In *In Spirit and in Truth: Essays on Theology, Spirituality and Embodiment,* edited by Phillip J. Anderson and Michelle Clifton Soderstrom, 241–256. Chicago, IL: Covenant Press, 2006.

———. "Mourning the Loss of Cultural Selfobjects: Black Embodiment and Religious Experience after Trauma." *Practical Theology* 1, no. 2 (2008): 1–20.

———. *Self, Culture and Others in Womanist Practical Theology.* New York: Palgrave Macmillan, 2011.

Snorton, Teresa A. "The Legacy of the African American Matriarch: New Perspectives for Pastoral Care." In *Through the Eyes of Women: Insights for Pastoral Care,* edited by Jeanne Stevenson Moessner, 50–56. Minneapolis, MN: Fortress Press, 1996.

Somé, Malidoma Patrice. *The Healing Wisdom of Africa: Finding Life Purpose through Nature, Ritual and Community.* New York: Jeremy P. Tarcher/Putnam, 1999.

Story, Rosalyn M. *And So I Sing: African American Divas of Opera and Concert.* New York: Harper Collins, 2000.

Swinton, John and Harriet Mowat. *Practical Theology and Qualitative Research.* New York: SCP Press, 2006.

Taylor, Susan L. *In the Spirit: Inspirational Writings of Susan L. Taylor.* New York: Amistad, 1999.

Thomas, Linda E. "Womanist Theology, Epistemology and a New Anthropological Paradigm." In *Living Stones in the Household of God: The Legacy and Future of Black Theology,* edited by Linda E. Thomas, 37–47. Minneapolis, MN: Augsburg Press, 2004.

Thomas, Stacey Floyd, ed. *Deeper Shades of Purple: Womanism in Religion and Society.* New York: New York University, 2006.

Townes, Emilie M., ed. *A Troubling in My Soul, Womanist Perspectives on Evil and Suffering.* Maryknoll, NY: Orbis Books, 1993.

———, ed. *Embracing the Spirit: Womanist Perspectives on Hope, Salvation, and Transformation.* Maryknoll, NY: Orbis, 1997.

———. *Womanist Ethics and the Cultural Production of Evil.* New York: Palgrave Macmillan, 2006.

Vanzant, Iyanla. *One Day My Soul Just Opened Up: 40 Days and Nights Towards Spiritual Strength and Personal Growth.* New York: Fireside Books, 1998.

Walker, Alice. *In Search of Our Mother's Gardens: Womanist Prose.* Orlando, FL: Harcourt Trade, 2004.

Walker, Elizabeth Johnson. "Counseling Grace: A Pastoral Theology." In *Women out of Order: Risking Change in a Multicultural World,* edited by Jeanne Stevenson Moessner and Teresa A. Snorton, 243–254. Minneapolis, MN: Fortress Press, 2009.

Walker-Barnes, Chanequa. "The Burden of the Strong Black Woman." *Journal of Pastoral Theology* 19, no. 1 (Summer 2009): 1–21.

Wallace, Beverly A. "A Womanist Legacy of Trauma, Grief and Loss: Reframing the Notion of the Strong Black Woman Icon." In *Women out of Order: Risking Change in a Multicultural World,* edited by Jeanne Stevenson Moessner and Teresa A. Snorton, 43–56. Minneapolis, MN: Fortress Press, 2009.

Wallace-Sanders, Kimberly. *Skin Deep, Spirit Strong: The Black Female Body in American Culture.* Ann Arbor: University of Michigan Press, 2002.

Watkins Ali, Carroll A. *Survival and Liberation: Pastoral Theology in African American Context.* St. Louis, MO: Chalice Press, 1999.

Wells, April C. "Pastoral Counseling as a Response to Intimate Violence and Institutional Abuse against African American Clergywomen in Black Church Leadership: A Womanist Pastoral Theological Model." ThD diss., Columbia Theological Seminary, 2007.

West, Traci C. *Wounds of the Spirit: Black Women and Resistance Ethics.* New York: New York University Press, 1999.

Westfield, N. Lynne. *Dear Sisters: A Womanist Practice of Hospitality.* Cleveland, OH: Pilgrim Press, 2001.

Williams, Delores S. "Womanist Theology: Black Women's Voices." *Christianity and Crisis* (March 2, 1987): 66–76.

———. "A Womanist Perspective on Sin." In *A Troubling in My Soul, Womanist Perspectives on Evil and Suffering,* edited by Emilie M. Townes, 130–149. Maryknoll, NY: Orbis Books, 1993.

Wimberly, Edward P. *African American Pastoral Counseling: The Politics of Oppression and Empowerment.* Cleveland, OH: Pilgrim Press, 2006.

Wyatt, Gail E., Jennifer Vargas Carmona, Tamra Burns Loeb, Armida Ayala, and Dorothy Chin. "Sexual Abuse." In *Handbook of Women's Sexual and Reproductive Health,* edited by Gina M. Wingood and Ralph J. DiClemente, 195–216. New York: Kluwer Academic/Plenum Publishers, 2002.

Yoder, Carolyn. *The Little Book of Trauma Healing.* Intercourse, PA: Good Books, 2005.

Name Index

Abelard, 19
Adams, Carol J., 179–80n5, 190nn32, 33
Anderson, Phillip J., 180n5
Angelou, Maya, 83
Anselm, 19
Arie, India, 60–1
Ayala, Armida, 190n31

Baby Suggs, holy, 129–35, 137, 142, 175
Basile, Kathleen C., 179nn1–4
Battle, Kathleen, 49
Berry, Jan, 141, 190n29
Black, Michele C., 179nn1–4
Blige, Mary J., 60
Boyd-Franklin, Nancy, 2, 181n6
Braxton, Toni, 60–1
Breiding, Matthew J., 179nn1, 4
Brooks Higginbotham, Evelyn, 7, 8, 181n12
Brown Douglas, Kelly, 16–18, 20, 119–23, 152, 153, 185n7, 180n5, 183nn25–7, 185n5
Bryson, Peabo, 27–8
Burns Loeb, Tamra, 190n31
Butler, Lee H. Jr., 188n15

Calvin, John, 19
Cannon, Katie, 188n16
Carr, Anne E., 179n5
Cavin, Adriana P., 187n11
Chen, Jieru, 179n1–4

Chin, Dorothy, 190n31
Clark-Hine, Darlene, 8, 160, 181n13, 192n25
Clifton Soderstrom, Michelle, 180n5
Coleman, Monica A., 180n5, 183n34, 188n21, 189n25
Cooper-White, Pamela, 17–18, 149, 156, 159, 181n5, 182n15, 183n28, 184n1, 190n30, 191nn1–5, 15, 192nn23, 28
Cozad Neuger, Christie, 156, 181n5, 191nn15, 16

DiClemente, Ralph J., 190n31
Dykstra, Craig, 187n10

Elliott Griffith, Mellissa, 188n22
Ely, Melvin Patrick, 6
Eugene, Toinette M., 179n5

Fortune, Marie, 144, 157, 158, 164, 179–80n5, 190nn32, 33, 34, 191n18, 192n28
Foster Boyd, Marsha, 126–8, 136, 147, 186n1, 188nn18, 19
Fowlkes, Martha, 165–6, 192n30
Fry Brown, Teresa L., 180n5, 187n9

Gilkes, Cheryl Townsend, 179n5
Gill-Austern, Brita, 186n4
Gilligan, Carol, 184n8
Glaz, Maxine, 180n5

Subject Index

abuse
  of adult, 1, 27, 34–5, 51, 58, 65,
    66, 69, 71, 89, 111, 117, 144,
    150, 161, 167, 182n16, 184n2
  breaking silence about, 3, 9, 28,
    32, 43, 57, 61, 69, 80, 85, 112,
    155–6
  of children, 31, 35, 45–7, 56, 61,
    66, 67–8, 84, 109, 112–13,
    115–16, 144, 149. *See also*
    incest, rape
  of children by children, 38, 39,
    41, 45–7, 67–8, 84, 115–16.
    See also incest, rape
  complicity of institutions in, 20,
    89, 112
  complicity of judicial community
    in, 87, 113
  complicity of practitioners in,
    129, 135
  complicity of relatives in, 26, 36,
    46, 56, 57, 69, 74, 112–13,
    163–4
  complicity of religion in, 2, 93–4,
    112, 190nn32, 33, 34
  coping strategies and, 32, 36,
    41, 43, 65–91, 117, 149, 151,
    163, 167, 171. *See also* spiritual
    practices
  depression and, 40, 41, 53, 68,
    78, 150–2
  effect on later intimate
    encounters, 69–70, 150

effects of (traumatic sequelae),
    22, 69, 146, 149–54, 160, 167
  emotional, 76, 110–11, 144,
    182n16
  by friend, 34, 74
  leading to more abuse, 70–1
  memory suppression of, 28–9, 32,
    39, 150, 154
  multigenerational, 31
  of power, 180n5
  of power in ritual, 22, 125, 143–4
  by relative, 26–31, 33, 34–5,
    38–40, 56, 65–9, 71
  religious justification of, 75, 95,
    112, 158
  resistance to, by church, 74–5,
    112, 113, 117, 119, 121, 123,
    132–4, 180n5
  resistance to, by employers, 18, 87–9
  resistance to, by relatives, 35, 46,
    47, 74
  specialness and, 67, 69
  stigma of, 35
  by stranger, 33–4, 51, 76, 181n7
acceptance
  by God, 29, 36–7, 55, 100, 103
affirmation, 60, 120, 136, 165
  as prayer, 104–5, 185n2.
    See also prayer
ancestors, 137, 138, 168–9
  naming of, 139, 141–2
  role of, 134, 138, 188n21, 189n25
  visits from, 168–9, 173

ritual, 125, 136–46
  detoxifying, 139
  Eight Bowls, 138–43
  healing, 136–47
  WomanistCare, 135–8, 147

sadism, 144
safe space, 36, 41, 78, 137, 146,
    175–6
salvation, 19–20, 85, 138
  through suffering, 153
  as transformation of
    sociopolitical structures, 20,
    186n1
  Womanist concept of, 20
Santeria, 50, 106–7
Sapphire, 5, 6, 7, 15, 134, 157
scapegoating
  of victim, 9, 157
self cohesion, 14–15
self expression, 43–4
self psychology, 9–16, 21
self-failure, 158–9
selfobject, 10–18, 66–9, 79, 184n1.
    See also cultural selfobject,
    empathy, Kohut
  cultural, 13–15, 89–90, 125,
    165 (people), 15 (symbols), 82
    (definition of), 82–90, 126,
    142, 161 (examples of), 90
    (therapist as). *See also* Cultural
    Craftswomen
  failing, 71, 163
  idealizing, 10–11, 66, 76–7,
    184n1
  language as, 15–16
  mirroring, 10–11, 14, 66, 74, 78,
    182n15
  negative, 15, 71
  positive, 90
  public policy as, 16
  transference, 66, 182n15
  transference repetition and, 71
  traumatic, 70–1

sewing, 88
  as coping strategy, 32, 88, 109, 112
  and reclaiming body, 109
  as spiritual practice, 62, 107–9, 136
  as truth-telling practice, 112
sex/love confusion, 70
sexual mythology, 183n24. *See also*
    Jezebel, Mammy, Sapphire
  political consequences of, 183n24
sexual violence, as rite of passage, 1
sexualization of poverty, 6–7, 135
shame, 23, 34, 44, 47–8, 50, 55,
    60, 68, 71, 80, 84, 85, 109–12,
    157–60, 166, 191n18. *See also*
    ostracism
  badness and, 110–12
  Buddhism and, 44, 100
  culture of, 159
  defensive responses to, 159–60
  empathy and, 160–7
  gender and, 159
  grace and, 172
  justice and, 109
  loss of connection and, 47, 112
  spiritual, 119, 160
  traumatic transference and, 149,
    156–8
sin, 17. *See also* crucifixion,
    defilement, incarnation
  flesh and, 17, 120–2
  as ontological, 17
  sexual, 191n18
  in systemic processes, 18, 135
  Womanist perspective of, 185n9
singing, 32, 48–9. *See also* grief,
    music, opera
  attitude and, 60–1
  as dispelling shame, 60–1
  as healing practice, 49, 53–4,
    56, 60
  as physical practice, 62
  as power, 60
  as spiritual practice, 107, 136
  as truth-telling practice, 45, 112

Printed in the United States of America